The Lord m

A Parish Priest Speaks with his People

A Fourth Selection

For Pauline
Love & God bless
R. Cormac

Cormac Rigby

Haddenham, Nov. 2006,

FAMILY PUBLICATIONS

OXFORD

ISBN 1-871217-60-1........ (hardback)
ISBN 1-871217-61-X........ (paperback)

by the same author
The Lord be with you
(also available on CD)
Lift Up Your Hearts
Let Us Give Thanks

*The author and the publishers wish to express their thanks
to those friends and parishioners who kindly allowed
the use of their illustrations in this book.*

*Front cover: Paschal Candle in Cardinal Newman's Oratory, Littlemore,
blessed by Fr Cormac, Easter Vigil 2006. Courtesy of the Sisters of the Work*

*Back cover: Fr Cormac in the sacristy at St William of York, Stanmore.
Photograph by Charles Maguire*

published by
Family Publications
6a King Street, Oxford, OX2 6DF
www.familypublications.co.uk

printed in England by
Cromwell Press, Trowbridge, Wilts.

Contents

Cormac Rigby ended twenty years at the BBC on 14th September 1985, presenting his final Last Night of the Proms.

He and Richard Baker were seen by viewers at the start of the second half – and then the streamers arrived. Photographs: Ken Corden.

Foreword

by Denis Riches

I was an enthusiastic listener to Radio 3 when I first came to know Cormac Rigby, and particularly enjoyed the way in which he presented his programmes, and appreciated how at the end of the evening he would say, "Good night, and God Bless!" Like so many people, I was surprised to hear in 1985 that he was leaving the BBC to become a Catholic priest – a big loss to the BBC, but a huge enrichment for the Church.

My wife Valerie and I became Catholics in 1982, and I started publishing Catholic books on retirement from the computer industry – in May 1988, the same month that Cormac was ordained priest by Cardinal Hume at Westminster Cathedral. We began receiving requests for books from this priest who was still only a name and a voice, until one day he wanted twenty Catechisms for the Maryvale Catechism course which he was planning for his parishioners at Ruislip. To save the postage he offered to collect the books, or if I cared to deliver them to his flat in Oxford, he would have the kettle on the boil.

It was the longest coffee break I've ever taken! We exchanged fascinating experiences of second careers, his as a Catholic priest, mine as a publisher and distributor of Catholic books. When I arrived back late for lunch, Valerie was intrigued by my experience and we arranged another meeting. We found that we shared so many interests – books, poetry, music, theatre, opera and ballet; and, of course, our faith.

We became firm friends and enjoyed regular visits to opera, theatre and ballet together. He sent us copies of the occasional parish newsletter, notes he had used on retreats and sermons. When I suggested that some of these should be published he dismissed the idea; and said that in any case, as a parish priest, he was far too busy.

In July 2003 he sent us a copy of the moving sermon in which he announced to his parishioners that he had been diagnosed as having cancer which had spread to his pelvis and spine, and that it had been agreed that he needed to retire from the parish in September. We drove to Stanmore the following Sunday to attend Mass at his church and found a shell-shocked parish – he was clearly a much loved priest.

Having read more of his well-crafted sermons – human, and yet so profound, and reaching out to Catholics at all levels of understanding – I again suggested some should be published, for the benefit of his family, friends and parishioners. He was still reluctant, and felt that the spoken word did not translate well into the written word. He always wrote out his sermons in his elegant long-hand on six or so sheets of A5, and they look like poetry; so I took his most recent sermon and typeset it so that it too looked like poetry, and gave it to him. He reflected and agreed, still somewhat reluctantly, to give it a go.

It was already October, and we felt that the future was uncertain. He selected thirty-three sermons from which we chose thirty, with appropriate photographs and illustrations. Archbishop Vincent Nichols, his former area bishop, wrote a foreword and we proceeded to publish *The Lord be with you* with all speed, in hardback and paperback. As pre-publicity he included a flyer with his Christmas cards, and by the time the books arrived in January we had so many orders that we had to print a further three thousand to satisfy demand from all over the world. The book received splendid reviews in the Catholic press and was chosen as book of the month by the Christian Book Club.

This all kept Fr Cormac very busy. We were delighted that excellent medical care and a world-wide blanket of prayer brought him remission from pain. People asked for more, and we published *Lift up your hearts* in September 2004, on the feast of St Cormac. We also spent two long mornings in a studio in London recording a selection from *The Lord be with you* onto CD, which was greatly appreciated by the many people who still remembered the golden voice from Radio 3. Feature articles about Fr Cormac appeared in the *Daily Telegraph* under the headline "Our finest Preacher?" and in the *Catholic Herald*; they were followed by enthusiastic reviews of the books, encouraging us to publish *Let Us Give Thanks* in November 2005.

In August 2005, I was myself diagnosed as having the same medical condition as Fr Cormac. When I told him, he responded: "Well, you've been praying every day for me, now it's my turn." His support and example have been a great source of encouragement, both to me and Valerie. We have the same oncologist, similar medication and pray that our remissions will continue.

And so we come to volume four, *The Lord my Light*. Of the sixty-plus books we have published, these have been the ones I have most enjoyed, and which have been the most spiritually enriching. It has been a great pleasure and privilege working so closely with Fr Cormac on these books. He contributes so much to the Church and to so many people, and has so much still to contribute. We hope that he will be spared for many more years and more volumes.

Oxford, July 2006

In his last term at school before starting at Oxford, Cormac Rigby in his natural habitat in the Senior Library at Merchant Taylors' School. Photograph: David Wallwork.

Introduction

Before the Preface at every Mass come three couplets of dialogue between celebrant and congregation. The Lord be with you . . . Lift up your hearts . . . Let us give thanks. And because I think of sermons as a sharing of life's experiences and a sharing of the faith, they seemed apt titles for collections of parish sermons.

Now that a fourth selection has been called for, I've turned to a phrase that has occurred daily in my life since I came up to Oxford and embarked on my commitment to daily Mass. It's the motto of the university itself: Dominus illuminatio mea. The Lord is my Light. The true student seeks enlightenment. The Creator's command Fiat Lux – let there be light – is the beginning of illumination. God himself is Lumen de lumine. "All that came to be was alive with his life, and that life was the light of men. The light shines on in the dark, and the darkness has never quenched it." (John 1:4,5).

In the paean of joy that is the Exultet at the Easter vigil, the priest asks that the Paschal candle be accepted:

Let it mingle with the lights of heaven
and continue bravely burning
to dispel the darkness of this night.

Dark night does come down on this rough-spoken world, and the banners of darkness are boldly unfurled. Fr Faber was right. There is in our society a gloom, a sense of life burning itself out and of individuals dying and fading to black, a world made of destructible dark materials.

The hope that springs eternal for Christians at Easter is regretfully denied. It becomes our task therefore to follow Cardinal Newman:

Lead kindly light, amid the encircling gloom.
Lead thou me on.

A century ago, the Jesuit Fr Joseph Rickaby published a volume of Oxford conferences under the title *The Lord my Light*. Earlier, on 23 November 1875, the year in which he received his red hat, the Archbishop of Westminster, Henry Edward Manning, preached a sermon at Oxford under the title *Dominus illuminatio mea*. It seems to me good to follow such precedents and to affirm the eternal light and the eternal life.

> May the Morning Star which never sets
> find this flame still burning:
> Christ, that Morning Star,
> who came back from the dead,
> and shed his peaceful light
> on all mankind.

Chapter 1

Love one another.

On Wednesday I celebrated my sixty-fifth birthday.
I'm now a pensioner.
I've reached my sell-by date – but not yet my use-by date.

I was reflecting during the week
on the circumstances of my arrival.
I wasn't really expected till the end of the month.
My mother's life was going on quite normally.
The 5th of May, in 1939, was a Friday, First Friday,
and so my mother walked the two miles down to the Church
in Rickmansworth for morning Mass.
She was a bit uncomfortable.
She'd fancied a pork chop on the Thursday evening
and it was repeating on her.
So after Mass, Mrs Kelly looked after her
and took her up to her own house for a cup of tea.
Mrs Kelly had by that time at least four children of her own
and quickly spotted that the indigestion
wasn't quite what my mother thought.
It wasn't a pork-chop. It was me.
And I arrived at quarter to nine that evening.
Thank goodness for Mrs Kelly.

How much we depend on the support of our neighbours,
on the practical help of our fellow-parishioners.
On Friday I was laughing about the pork-chop episode
with one of Mrs Kelly's daughters.
She was about four at the time, and she's now a retired G.P.
Like her mother, she's an active participator
in the life of her present parish.

We met up again a few years ago –
the children of those two mothers, and enjoyed the links
that connected us through the life of the parish.
Such connections mean a great deal to me
– the Not-Quite-a-Pork-Chop.

It's in details like this
that the real history of Christianity is written.
The real history isn't all bishops and theologians;
it's also the practising believers – us,
the church, the day-to-day Christians.

Bernadette – née Kelly – and I have both shared
one great joy: the joy of taking Communion
to the sick and housebound.
The body-language of the Blessed Sacrament is tremendous.
"My coming among you wasn't just a historical one-off,"
says the Lord. "I didn't come on earth just once,
two thousand years ago,
and then retreat into eternity.
I rose in my body to the right hand of the Father;
I ascended into heaven,
but I did not leave you without my presence among you.
From the moment of the Incarnation
I am God with you.
I am with you as the man called Jesus;
I am with you through my death and Resurrection.
And I am with you *beyond* my bodily Ascension.
I am with you whenever you break bread
and do this in memory of me."

Nothing in our faith is more tremendous
than this fact of his abiding presence.
Nothing – as John Betjeman once reminded us –

> Can with this single Truth compare –
> That God was Man in Palestine
> And lives to-day in Bread and Wine.

That eucharistic presence,
that sacrament of God's visible love is the heart of our faith.

Bernadette and I shared many memories of the elderly,
the sick, the injured, the disturbed, the senile,
who were able to recognise in that simple circle of bread
My Lord and My God.
And it struck me afresh as we were talking that the Church
is not just an accumulation of people praising God together.

The Church is Jesus himself, still among his people,
still nourishing them,
still reinforcing their love for one another.
The theological phrase is "The mystical body of Christ."
That's us: the members of the body of the Lord.
And so it inevitably follows that we should love one another.

We gather together, conscious that we
are not a mere random selection of individuals,
but interdependent parts of his glorious risen Body.
He is the head, we are the members.

We look up at that visible Real Presence,
Emmanuel, God among us, and we say My Lord and My God,
and we feel his footfall on our tongue or on our hand
as he steps into our hearts.

I thought of those two mothers sixty-five years ago:
fellow parishioners, friends, bonded together on
that First Friday of my life – and I thank God
that down through two thousand years
the faithful have gathered to follow
that new commandment given to the apostles
at the Last Supper:

Love one another;
just as I have loved you, you also must love one another;
by this love you have for one another,
everyone will know that you are my disciples.

Auntie Mary, my Godmother, flew over from Canada to be at my ordination in 1988. In 1935 she had been my mother's bridesmaid. Auntie Mary and Mother relax in the playground of Westminster Cathedral Choir School after the ceremony.

Chapter 2

The Lord is close to all who call him from their hearts.

I had a great holiday.
The first eight or nine days were pure relaxation.
I was over in West Cork and then moved on up to Connemara.
And then for the last couple of days I was in Leitrim,
where my grandfather came from:
a town called Drumshanbo.
It was always my mother's favourite place,
and when she died, it was there, in 1999,
that we scattered her ashes.

Late on my first afternoon there I wandered up to the church
where my mother's three closest friends rest in adjacent graves.
They were friends for eighty years and more:
Molly and Frances and Florrie.
Molly and Florrie died within the same week in 1984;
Frances died a year or two before my mother.
I stood by the graves and thought gratefully
of those long years of friendship.
Frances had a large family, but neither Molly nor Florrie
had children. Florrie was godmother to my sister –
a kind and faithful godmother.
For years, Mrs Cunningham's shop and pub was the busiest
in the High Street. She was a canny businesswoman
but with an immensely kindly heart.
A good godmother to have.

And thinking of my sister's godmother,
I thought of my own too. Auntie Mary.
She was my mother's oldest and closest friend in St Helens –
Mary Shiel. There were photos of her in Mother's album
and she was really beautiful.

She was Mother's bridesmaid in 1935
and so when I was born in 1939 Mary was asked
to be my godmother and I've always been proud of her.
She married and had her own family and was widowed
for many years. She went to live in Canada and
I last saw her in 1988 when she came over for my ordination.

They were well into their eighties then, and it became a joke
that whenever the question was asked: what happened
to so and so? And what happened to her brother?
the answer was always the same – she died; he died.
In the end they were laughing at themselves
– the great survivors.

I had a letter from Auntie Mary's granddaughter recently –
Auntie Mary was worried because she hadn't heard from me
since Christmas.
I sat down *at once* to write to her – thinking how lucky I was
at the age of sixty-three to have a godmother who was still
wanting to know how I was getting on!
And as I stood beside those graves in Drumshanbo
I thought of how important my mother's closest friends
had become to me, and in particular
how much my godparents mattered to me.

Early next morning in Roscommon I had a phone call
from St Helens to let me know that Auntie Mary had died.

It was so early in the morning
that I was able to offer my Mass that day for her.
Lovely, I thought, that I'd been thinking of her
just as she was going to meet her maker.
Wonderful – providential – that on the very day
that I was going down to Lough Allen
where my mother's ashes were scattered, I should hear
the news of her dearest friend's arrival in heaven.
I could imagine the welcome Mary had and the catching up.

The choosing of godparents is a most important decision.
Sometimes, alas, all sorts of silly social considerations
are allowed to creep in.
Of course it is a great honour to be a godparent
but it's a great responsibility too. A role model.
An actively interested extra parent. A safety net.
A longstop. Responsibility for spiritual well-being.
With Auntie Mary living in Canada I didn't see her often,
but I was constantly aware of her
and at my ordination, she was there.

The sacraments of the Church are visible events
in the life of the soul.
At our baptism, the role of parent is extended
to two or more others.
And – in the words of the ceremony itself –
they must be ready to help the mother and father
in their duty as Christian parents.

You must make it your constant care to bring him up
in the practice of the faith. See that the divine life
which God gives him is kept safe from the poison of sin
to grow always stronger in his heart.

And when the baptismal candle is lit the priest says

Parents *and* godparents this light is entrusted to you
to be kept burning brightly.

God bless those three wonderful friends who drew me to pray
that afternoon above the town.
And God bless those two ladies, Grace and Mary,
the bride and bridesmaid, my mother and my godmother
whose friendship dominated my thoughts that evening
in Drumshanbo. The light *was* kept burning brightly
all through those wonderfully long lives.

Whenever I talk with parents about the baptism
of their baby, I look forward to hearing why
the godparents have been chosen.

17

Motherhood and fatherhood in the spirit
are so important to us.

And by the same token when our confirmation candidates
are choosing for themselves who will be their sponsor,
it is an extension and development of that same role –
choosing someone who will help to keep the light of faith
burning brightly.
To share values. To share hopes.
To be a source of strength and resolution.

I felt the Lord very close to me
as I spoke to him from a full heart
thanking him for my godmother's life.

I wish that all the babies I baptise
and that all our confirmation candidates
will find similar inspiration in their godparents and sponsors.

Chapter 3

On the same night that he was betrayed
the Lord Jesus took some bread . . .

It's the chronology of events that fascinates me.
Jesus died on the cross
– and then he was buried
and then on the third day he rose again.

And *then*, surely, he would gather the disciples together
for a party, a celebration, maybe kill the fatted calf.

My son who was lost is found.
My son who was dead is risen.

The newly-risen Lord would surely want to put fresh heart
into his troops, and to explain to them that he was
going to leave them again, and therefore wanted now
to brief them about how, after his Ascension,
he would continue to stay close to them.

But actually it didn't happen like that.
The Big Meal didn't happen *after* the Resurrection
– it took place *before* the Passion even began.
If it *had* happened afterwards,
they'd have known what they were celebrating:
a death *and* a resurrection.
But it didn't.
Jesus used the pretext of a Passover meal
to gather them together *before* the great betrayal
and the trials and the terrible Passion.
The Great Supper wasn't a celebration after the events.
It was a prelude and its significance couldn't possibly
have been understood by the apostles at the time.
The gesture of washing their feet – *that* was easy enough.
He'd spoken before about how they should behave towards

one another. Washing the feet was to demonstrate service
and to show how perfect his love was.

But the bread? The wine? The body, the blood?
Do it in memory of me – what was all that about?
At the time it was frankly incomprehensible.
It didn't fit the pattern. It didn't make sense.
It wasn't until long afterwards that they understood
what was going on.
He was deliberately planting in their collective consciousness
a sequence of events which they would never forget.

On that same night that he was betrayed,
he leapt beyond the Crucifixion and Resurrection
and instituted the means by which his death,
his sacrifice, would become sacramentally present
to succeeding generations.
Paul spelt it out years later to the Corinthians:
"Until the Lord comes, therefore,
every time you eat this bread and drink this cup,
you are proclaiming his death."

If he'd had a great bean-feast after the first Easter,
it would clearly be proclaiming his *Resurrection*.
That wasn't what he wanted.
The Last Supper is not primarily about resurrection;
it's about death; it's about *sacrifice*.
It's tied in of course with the associations of
the Passover Meal – the lamb killed,
the lintels of the doors marked with blood,
the angel of death passing over the people.
From the lamb sacrificed,
the mind goes to the lamb self-immolating:
the sacrifice that exists in the dimension of eternity,
the eternal self-sacrifice of the Son
offered eternally to the Father.
Whenever we re-enact the Last Supper

we are tapping in to that eternal self-sacrifice.
It happens, continuingly, in the eternal present.
Historically, it happened on the cross on Calvary
– and before, note *before* that moment in history,
it happened sacramentally.
That's why the chronology is so odd.
We proclaim the death of the Lord and we proclaim it *before*
the historical moment when it happens.

Usually in human affairs, things happen in a certain sequence
and are commemorated later.
The Last Supper turns such human logic on its head,
and we join Jesus as he offers himself in sacrifice
before the death on the Cross.
Our conclusion from this is that the Mass
is not just a commemoration of an historical meal
recorded in scripture, but something much more than that.

It is the eternal presence of the Sacrifice
which in historical terms had not yet taken place.
The Mass *is* the Sacrifice,
not repeated over and over and over again
but offered continuously in eternity:
the Sacrifice of the Son to the Father.
The Mass is not a commemorative meal,
not a celebratory banquet – and the focus is *not* a table.
It is a sacrifice and the focus is an altar.

Certainly Christ *is* food and drink to us; we take Christ
into our hearts and make him part of our chemistry.
But it is *his* action, not ours, that really matters.
On the Cross he died for our sins.
His love for the Father, and for creation,
is so great that he accepts us as his siblings
and offers himself to redeem us.
His is the action of the Mass; our participation certainly
nourishes us, but it is *his* action which saves us.

It is significant that when the risen Jesus joined
his disciples in the Upper Room, they realised that
he still bore the wounds of his Passion.
They are an essential part of the glory of the Risen Christ.
The wounded Christ is the source of our forgiveness.
We are the beneficiaries of his sacrifice.

The Mass is far more than a meal; it is the shedding of blood.
When the soldier approached the already dead Jesus,
and pierced his side, there was no more blood to flow.
The sacrifice was complete, *is* complete.
The blood of the Lamb has washed away our sins.

> Blood of my Saviour, bathe me in thy tide,
> Wash me with water flowing from thy side.

We need to focus afresh on the Mass
as the present experience of the eternal sacrifice.
This is the very heart of our salvation.

I was a little boy of four when Pius XII reminded us
of its significance in *Mystici Corporis Christi:*

> As the divine Redeemer, when he was dying on the Cross,
> offered himself to the Father as the head of the whole
> human race so, in this 'clean oblation' [of the Mass]
> he offers to the heavenly Father not only himself,
> as Head of the Church but in himself also his mystical
> members, for he encloses them all, even the weak
> and frail among them, most lovingly in his heart.

That is where we find ourselves at Mass:
enclosed most lovingly in his heart.

*Sermon preached in Cardinal Newman's Oratory, Littlemore,
Maundy Thursday, 2006.*

Chapter 4

Happy are you . . .

I could add another Beatitude.
Happy are those who know who they are.
I'm Cormac Rigby.
My father was Edward, 'Ted',
a pattern-maker from St Helens,
a painstaking perfectionist,
a convert.
My mother is Grace,
a teacher, also from St Helens,
a lover of life,
and deeply devoted to the faith of her fathers.

My father's father was a brewer's drayman,
who married Sarah, a placid and hardworking woman,
a gentle Methodist.
My mother's father was a McCormack,
an insurance salesman from Co Leitrim,
who as a young boy saw his family evicted
and their house torched by the landlord's men,
and he married a Kavanagh from Mayo,
a political firebrand whose whole life in local politics
was dedicated to the poorly housed.

So I know who I am, and I know where I come from.
I look into myself
and I see some of the characteristics of my parents.
I know the streams of history that have flowed through
into my life and although I'm unique,
I know and understand a lot of what makes me unique.
Happy the man who can set himself in context.

And it is precisely for that reason that marriage is so crucial.
We get used to thinking of marriage as a bilateral relationship
– seeing each couple linked together
in a duo of emotional importance.
Marriage *is* about couples – but it's much more than that.
The Church sees it as part of a deeper reality.
Marriage is the giving of love from one to another
and it is intended as the context for creation.
We are the inheritors of life, not just from our parents
but from *their* parents and their parents' parents . . .
And that is why the Church is so totally opposed to
the transmission of life in any context other than marriage.

Sperm banks, in vitro fertilisation
– they all seem so progressive and so technically masterful,
but they rob the individual of his awareness
of his place in the continuity of life.
It seems an act of charity, almost, to make it possible
for a woman deprived of motherhood to be given
the semen of a stranger and enabled to give life to a child.
In the short-term it is hard to resist that emotional 'plus'
– but there are two inseparable 'minuses'.

The first is that in the achieving of one successful birth,
other fertilisations are made, and aborted.
There is in that process a sort of survival of the fittest,
and the lives of potential siblings are terminated,
as brutally as a baby cuckoo turfs the nestlings
of its adoptive parents out of the nest.
Life for one artificially created human
occurs at the expense of death for others.

The second minus
is that the child who is born as a consequence
of such a process can only draw on the love of one parent,
and may well never know the other half of his inheritance.

The child comes into the world already bereaved
– not knowing the reality of half his story
and concerned perhaps that that unknown history
may have a darker side.

Today is St Valentine's Day, and what a lot of gooey slush comes
with that distortion of what love is all about.
This is a week focussing on the institution of marriage,
and we all know how arguments of personal freedom
and fulfillment are used to challenge
the church's ideal of marriage.
Neither the bogus romanticism of Valentine's day
nor the dubious arguments of liberalism
really undermine confidence in that ideal.

If marriage achieves its purpose,
the thread of continuity becomes apparent
– and how worthwhile it is
to achieve not only the fulfilment of the love of man and wife
but also the recognition by their children
of the unique complexity of all they inherit.

We see this so often in the experience of adopted children
who later meet their birth-mother.
It does not undermine love and gratitude
towards adoptive parents – but it helps the individuals
to know more deeply who they really are.

Happy are those who know who they are
and happy are those who *enable* them to know who they are.

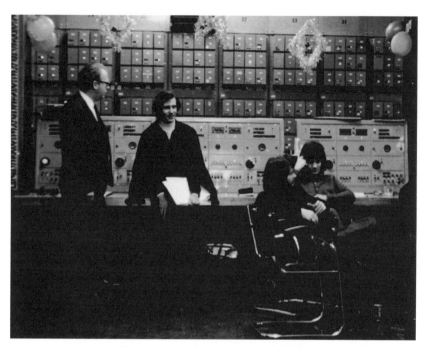

Each radio network had its own continuity studio, contained within the London Control Room, in Broadcasting House Extension. On the other side of the glass were the TOs – technical operators – colleagues who often became good friends. On Christmas Eve 1971 I was in Radio 4 Con from 3pm to 6pm (which included the live carols from King's Cambridge), then had supper in the canteen with the duty newsreader, Peter Donaldson, before returning to Continuity until a late close-down. Radio 4 had Big Ben at midnight, followed by a live Midnight Communion from Cardiff. So it was a late close-down.

"As we close, I know my own family will probably be home now from Midnight Mass, so I wish them as I wish you, a happy and enjoyable day. To you listening alone this Christmas Day, I wish the peace which the shepherds watching alone on the hillsides above Bethlehem were the first to hear about and recognise: that peace, this Christmas.

"At seven minutes past one, this is Cormac Rigby in Broadcasting House wishing you Goodnight and God bless. Good night!"

Then I finished my logging and set up the next morning's jobs and popped in to wish Keith Skues a happy Christmas and then stayed chatting with TOs in the Control Room for an hour before crossing the road to the Langham for a short night's kip.

Photograph shows Assistant Technical Operations Manager (ATOM) John Bradburn, Cormac Rigby, Mike Davies, Neil Espley.

26

Chapter 5

The Continuity of God's love

Continuity. The word moved into the centre of my life when I joined the BBC in 1965. Within the London Control Room, were the network continuities: Home, Light and Third, and now the Music Programme.

The formal task of continuity was to deliver to the listeners what *Radio Times* had promised. The underlying task was to do so in a sympathetic way which allowed each listener to think that the individual programmes were an experience shared – and enjoyed – by listener and announcer alike. Tact, respect, tone of voice, good humour, clarity and deft perception of the material itself were all desiderata. Respect for the output meant great care had to be taken to move, not seamlessly but appropriately from one thing to another. I recall how Patricia Hughes, towards the end of the relay of the service for the Olympic athletes assassinated in Munich, realised that there would be a considerable under-run, and chose Bruch's *Kol Nidrei* as the bridge between that emotional live broadcast and the next scheduled programme. I remember my adrenalin flowing in live interval readings, and to this day I am proudest of Gray's *Elegy Written in a Country Churchyard* and Oscar Wilde's *The Selfish Giant*. But equally one took pride in the solving of problems before they became audible. What struck the listener as an uneventful shift had very often been an exhausting sequence of avoiding actions.

The more I reflected on the requirements of continuity the more it appealed to the historian in me. This day's work is part of the continuous creation of the character of a network. This small decision of mine is an element in the development of an Idea of broadcasting. This moment exists between the chronicled history

that had made the Third Programme the envy of the world
and a future of continuing awareness, insights, pleasures
and life-enhancing experiences.

I became more aware of my personal accumulation of experiences.
They had begun with quiet evenings in a fellow-undergraduate's
rooms, learning to appreciate his collection of records.
Later, sitting through rehearsals
before live-concerts brought me greater understanding
of how musical performances come together.

The writing, paring and endless refining of scripts,
the constant efforts to be succinct and accurate,
the most effective length of a pause, the awareness
of silence within speech – nothing was ever wasted.
That became part of my perception too:
nothing was ever wasted. The intimate familiarity
with the network led to a wider sense of continuity.

Hearing certain near-perfect pieces in different performances
created an awareness of an Ideal performance.
Not as an actual event but as a conceivable reality,
comprehended in my mind as the ultimate possibility.
I made the leap of perception that the ultimate exists:
more than the sum of all the parts of my experience,
but a mystery, the awareness of which was within my grasp.
Not perfectly perceived, but its existence permitting
no doubt of its value. If that is true of music,
then I could hold firmly and absolutely an Idea of God.
The one ultimate fullness.
The Ultimate Perfect Continuity.
The ever-present Continuum of God.

I came to realise from my own experience that it is not
just wishful thinking, not me stretching after an Ideal,
not just me in quest of God, but God initiating the whole process
by seeking out me. Well, he would, wouldn't he, if he is

the Ultimate Perfection of Love?
Just as the great artist plays in such a sublime way that
it seems that he is playing only for you,
the Ultimate Love sustains life in everything for its own sake.
"Thou art careful and tender to each of the beings that
Thou hast created," wrote Newman, "as if it were
the only one in the whole world."
Uniquely loved. That's the truth of it. The Love that created us
is inexhaustible and never-ending. Newman again: "Thou never
wilt forsake me. I may securely repose upon Thee. Sinner as I am,
nevertheless, while I am true to Thee, Thou wilt still and to the end,
be superabundantly true to me."

The continuity of God's love for me emerges in all the loving and
thoughtful intricacy of his work. My relationship with him may
have stops and starts, high points and deep lows,
but just as his continuity of creation of me keeps me in being,
so his continuity of love of me keeps me undaunted.
I have so much to explore in the infinite creation of God;
I have so much joy to experience in the infinite love of God.
I am uniquely loved, because he made me in his own image.
And because he is immortal, so am I.

Could a creature be uniquely loved and then discarded?
My first experience of death's assault on love came in 1964.
And in the sharpened perception of grief in bereavement
I saw clearly that it is impossible for love to terminate love.
Separated I might be, bereft never.
The total love which finds its historical expression on Calvary,
the sacrificial offering of the life of God-made-man,
is never going to cease to love.
Ceasing to love would be an unimaginable break in the
continuity of God. Easter is therefore the triumph
of the continuity of God's love for each one of us.

Pope Pius XII 1939-58

Blessed John XXIII 1958-63

Pope Paul VI 1963-78

Pope John Paul II 1978-2005

Chapter 6

Was it not ordained that the Christ should suffer?

So we are without a Pope.
The see of Rome is empty.
And that's not how a monarchy works.
The Queen is dead; long live the King.
The moment the present Queen dies
– and may it still be a very long way ahead –
her son becomes King. There is no gap.

Nor is there a real gap in a parliamentary democracy.
When the election results were declared,
Mr Major set off for Buckingham Palace to resign his office,
and the Queen did not delay in sending for Mr Blair.
We assume that there will be continuity
both in our head of state and in our head of government.

The Church does not behave in the same way.
There is a real historical gap, a *caesura*,
a lull between two pontificates.
It happens in all dioceses,
as I do not need to tell *you* in this diocese of Northampton.
Of course most of the everyday business of the diocese
carries on. But there are some things *only* a Pope can do.
And that makes us acutely aware of *sede vacante*,
the gap, the lull.
And that is very necessary because it makes us *all* take stock.
Not just the Cardinals, but you and me.
We have suffered with our dying Pope
and we have mourned his passing
and we have read the obituaries.
And now we have to think and pray.

We have to pray that the Cardinals will choose
a good successor to John Paul II.

I have no doubt that the Cardinals themselves
have been thinking about it for some months.
And whenever they bump into one another around the globe,
they'll have been assessing one another.
He runs his diocese brilliantly;
he's great with the media;
he's really concerned with doctrinal firmness;
he's working flat out for the cancelling of Third World debt;
he's a terrific writer;
he spends a full month every year on retreat;
he's an amazing linguist.
And I daresay there might even be
the odd negative assessment too. That's their job.
If we're going to get the right man to succeed Karol Wojtyla,
the Cardinals have got to know
one another's strengths and weaknesses.

The Church isn't a democracy.
Giving every member a vote wouldn't serve a useful purpose
because our perceptions would be so superficial;
our 'favourite' would not necessarily be the best man.

In 1978 when Paul VI died and then his successor
John Paul I died after only thirty-three days as pope,
I was working in BBC Radio and was covering
all eventualities in the broadcast coverage
of funerals, conclaves, elections and installations.
My job was to prepare for unexpected hiccups
– the lines going down – that sort of thing:
the belt and braces activities that listeners take for granted.
One of the contingency plans I made was if there were
to be a delay going over to Rome at the very start.

So I dug around in the archives to find old recordings
of the proclamations of new popes and put them together
with a linking commentary.
A ten-minute package of papal polyfilla.

What intrigued me was the reaction of the crowds
in St Peter's Square.
Habemus Papam. Mighty cheer.
Eminentissimum ac Reverendissimum Dominum,
Dominum – then came the Christian name of the new pope.

In 1939 *Eugenium* was instantly recognised by the crowd:
Eugenio Pacelli, the old pope's right hand man
and the clear favourite, probably elected on the first ballot.
A terrific roar of approval before they could proceed
with the announcement of the surname.
But in 1958 when Pius XII died, the Christian names
of his successor were *Angelum Josephum,* and you could hear
the crowd wondering who on earth he was.
When he in his turn died, the greatly-loved Pope John XXIII,
there was again a clear favourite.
So when Cardinal Ottaviani announced the new pope as
Johannem Baptistam, the crowd erupted into a huge cheering
for Cardinal Montini who took the name Paul VI.

On his passing in 1978 there was a completely different response –
a much more muted response – to *Albinum.*
And a few weeks later when John Paul I had so suddenly died,
not only did the crowd not recognise *Karolum*
– they didn't recognise *Wojtyla* either !
It was only when the Polish Pope emerged and spoke
to them himself in Italian that the real cheers began.

So you see, the people would be pretty hopeless as electors.
We need our new shepherd to be chosen for us
by the men who really *know* those involved.
But that doesn't diminish our task.

Our task is to pray that the Holy Spirit will guide them
in their choice, to ensure that our new Holy Father
will be a man of deeds, not just words.

John Paul II was brilliant in so many ways:
teaching, preaching, strengthening us.
But he knew that actions speak louder then words.
He came to Britain even though there was a war on.
He went to Jerusalem and stood in visible prayer
at the Western Wall to begin the healing of the long rift
between the people of the old and new covenants.

And in his last days and hours, he demonstrated
the absolute value of a human life,
determined not to waste a minute of his allotted span.
He knew how inconvenient the elderly are
and how impatient western society is
of their infirmities.
His actions simply said: I am as much me
in my trembling infirmity as I was in my vigorous strength.
I speak as eloquently in my frustrated silence
as I did in my dramatic oratory.
Was it not ordained that the Christ should suffer?
The value of suffering is not to be gainsaid.
Nothing of human life is wasted if we are resolved to use it.

Let us pray that this pause between two papal reigns
will enable the Cardinals to consider our pastoral needs
– and enable us to consider them too.

Chapter 7

Neither do I condemn you

How do you start to love God?
How can you feel any powerful emotion
about a distant Being far beyond the stars?
To be perfectly honest
I've never been able to *love* a pure spirit.
Admire, yes; worship, certainly; but not *love*.
You love a person, not an ideal.
Which is precisely why God in his infinite wisdom
felt it necessary to reach out to humanity with human arms.
I learnt to know and love God through his incarnate Son,
the Word made flesh, the Jesus who lived and died for me.
Faced with concepts like eternity and infinity
I stand in awe but they don't inspire love.
It's Jesus who does that.

The mind of the creator is beyond my grasp
but the sacred heart of Jesus beats in time with my own heart.
In other words, you have to start from what you know.
It's in your own experience of love that you begin,
just begin to understand what infinite love might be.
The poet William Cory found it impossible
to begin from a distant Being beyond the stars:

> You say there is no substance here,
> One great reality above:
> Back from that void I shrink in fear,
> And child-like hide myself in love.

I share his inability to connect with an abstract being,
but when I hide myself in love, child-like,
I hear the voice of Jesus reassuring me:

"Anyone who does not welcome the kingdom of God
like a little child will never enter it."
It's the here and now humanity of Jesus
which opens up my approach to God;
it's the here and now beauty of the world
which opens up my mind to paradise.
     All the beauty I see he has given to me
     and his giving is gentle as silence.
That persuasive hymn of Estelle White
expresses it beautifully.
The beauty I can genuinely love here gives me access
to the God who is ultimate Beauty.
But of course there's more to life than beauty.
William Wordsworth experienced
a "bliss ineffable" when he felt
"the sentiment of Being spread o'er all that moves."
But the time of life when bliss is ineffable
– though undoubtedly intense –
is, in my experience, rather short.
That sort of elevated thought tends to vanish
like the Cheshire cat.
Human love is not continuous bliss,
it's full of ups and downs,
full of venturings and mistakes,
sometimes deliriously happy, sometimes deeply frustrating,
always prone to wishful thinking and misguided experiments.

We are never more vulnerable than when we fall in love.
It is *so* difficult to get it right.
But the best of our loves,
the love that survives disappointment and rejection,
the love that inspires the rest of life,
the love that endures when lesser loves melt in the sunshine,
the wondrous immortal diamond of true love

opens our perceptions
to the Love of all Love, the God who is Love.
We do our best to love what and who are most worthy
of our love but inevitably we make mistakes.
And that is why the third verse of that hymn is so essential.
Just loving the beautiful is not enough.

There've been times when I've turned from his presence,
And I've walked other paths, other ways
But I've called on his name in the dark of my shame,
And his mercy is gentle as silence.

Yes, yes, yes. That is ultimate love.
His mercy is gentle as silence.

A mistake was made by the woman taken in adultery,
a serious error of judgment. It hurt.
And they were so eager to rub her nose in it.
All those perfection-worshipping, loveless people
were prepared to stone her.
And he sat silently, doodling in the dust with his finger.
And she looked at him, waiting for his condemnation.
And he said not a word to her.
He looked instead at all those self-righteous worshippers
of abstracts, her accusers, and he said:
"If there is one of you who has not sinned
let him be the first to throw a stone at her."
He understood intuitively how hard it is to love blamelessly,
how easy to make mistakes.
The righteous melted away, baffled by his understanding.
Only their intended victim remained,
and only then did he speak to her:
"Neither do I condemn you."
And his mercy was gentle as silence.

The portrait of John Goad is the frontispiece of his Astro-Meteorologica. *Photograph: courtesy of British Museum.*

Chapter 8

A saint of strifeless love

The Reverend John Goad had good reason to be grateful
for the restoration of the monarchy in 1660. For in the
entourage of the Queen Mother, Henrietta Maria, was the
priest who in December, 1660, received him into the Church
at Somerset House.

It was the turning point in that holy and learned man's
long and useful life which reflects only too well the turmoil
of the times. He was born in London in 1616 and went from
Merchant Taylors' School to St John's College, Oxford,
where in due course he became a fellow.

This was during the civil war, and Goad won fame by
continuing to hold divine service in the church of St Giles,
a college living which he then held, while the rebel cannon
were pounding away outside. It was very typical of Goad
to put the service of God before all other considerations.
In 1646 he became Vicar of Yarnton, a living which he
held on to with some difficulty during the Commonwealth.

His fellowship was taken away from him when President
Baylie of St John's was ejected for supporting the King,
a setback which deprived Goad of the opportunity to return
to his old school as an examiner of the scholars
proposed for entry from the school to the college.

During the Republic he earned a little extra by private teaching,
among his pupils being the famous historian
of the University, Anthony Wood, who describes him
as "an exceedingly loving and tender man."

The evidence for his conversion in 1660 comes in fact
from Wood, who knew him so well. Although it has been

challenged on the grounds that sermons preached by Goad
later than this were not Catholic in tone,
the evidence of Wood is preferable.

On 12 July 1661 Goad proceeded to take the mastership
of his own old school, Merchant Taylors', a position
he was to hold for nearly twenty years.
The school was in no wise a Catholic school. Its statutes
demanded that regular instruction should be given in the
Catechism of the Church of England. And Goad, although
himself unable to accept those beliefs, was true to his terms
of reference when he accepted the post.
His honour in this respect was matched by the success of
his teaching. He attracted many by his own reputation as
a schoolmaster and carried the school through the difficult
days of reaction after the King's return. His school was
one of the first to end the anti-Puritan excesses
that followed the Restoration and return to a normal life.

One of his first concerns was to see that the boys were
adequately provided with books; he is rightly regarded
as the founder of the excellent school library, and we may
detect there the only hint of his faith.
Among the books that survive from that time are several
that would indicate a Catholic interest, including, for example,
some of the scientific works of the Jesuit Kircher. They reflect
more than his Catholicism however, for he was himself
a well-known amateur scientist in his spare time.
His main interest was in meteorology, and the Bodleian Library
still possesses the diary he kept of the weather in London
from 1677 to 1679.
His observations, combined with his excellent scriptural
knowledge, bore fruit in the work which won him the most
admiration, the *Astro-Meteorologica*. This was based,
as the author claims, on thirty years observations.
But all this does not mean that he was a dull schoolmaster;

far from it. On one occasion he produced a school play, Beaumont and Fletcher's *Love's Pilgrimage*, which cost the school seven pounds ten shillings and ninepence. Disaster overtook the school in 1666, when the great fire of London raged through the city, destroying much that was valuable as well as much that needed clearing away. Merchant Taylors' was destroyed on the first afternoon of the conflagration, which lasted altogether for three days.

The bibliophile headmaster made great efforts to save what he could, and had no hesitation in risking his own life and property in order to save the precious books in the newly established library.

When the fire had done its work he tried to keep as much education going as possible, teaching for a year in an unknown place in the ruins and then moving into a disused grammar school until his own school could be rebuilt.

One may reasonably suppose that the master's Catholicism was an open secret. There were many who were known to be Catholics but who could not in those dangerous days make a public profession.

It was the sort of news that spreads along the gossip vines, and we may be sure that the young boy who entered the school five years after Goad's appointment would be aware of it. And we may be sure that when he was expelled a year later, Master Titus Oates remembered it and stored it up in his evil mind for future reference.

Opportunity came in 1681 when the country was panic-stricken by the alleged Popish Plot 'revealed' by Oates. In the anti-Catholic hysteria that was to sweep so many innocent Catholics to death, a complaint was made by the Grand Jury of London that Goad was a papist.

He was not the only victim from the school: Oates also took action against Isaac Backhouse, some-time master of Wolverhampton Grammar School. Backhouse was also a former pupil of Goad, and perhaps it was the action against the loved headmaster that moved Backhouse to call after Oates in St James's Park, "There goes Oates, that perjured rogue."

Oates, at the height of his power, had no hesitation in starting proceedings for libel.

The Merchant Taylors' Company was reluctantly forced to take action against Goad, and though the master was so well-loved a figure, and the proceedings were spun out to give him every chance, there was no hope that he would deny his Catholicism.

In that atmosphere of fear and hatred, no Catholic thus attacked could have remained inviolate, however esteemed. In addition to this there was the added hazard of the ambition of one of his accusers, Dr John Owen, who was eager to secure the headmastership for his nephew, one John Hartcliffe.

The forces ranged against Goad were too strong, and his twenty years service went for nothing. On April 13, 1681, he was dismissed for being "popishly and erroneously effected." But the Company was too grateful to allow him to go as abruptly as that. A fortnight later they voted him a gratuity, "£70 as a gratuity, including the £10 by him paid for taxes, trophies, and chimney-money."

Even so the dismissal caused many complaints. Several of the parents were disgusted and took their boys away when Hartcliffe became Headmaster, and instead sent their sons to the little private school that Goad opened in Piccadilly. He taught privately for the rest of his life, combining this with his writing and scientific enquiry.

In 1685 James II came to the throne; Catholicism became temporarily less dangerous and the old septuagenarian made public acknowledgment that he was a Catholic.

He had only three more years to live, during which time
he saw the last Catholic king forced into exile, and
a new dynasty established by parliamentary invitation.

He died in London on 28 October 1689, and was buried
where he was baptised in St Helen's, Bishopsgate.

After his death the little work that had occupied his
last years appeared in print. It was a practical
Latin vocabulary, "being the best and easiest Method
yet extant for young Beginners to attain to the knowledge
of the Latin tongue."

Also in the year after his death there appeared an anonymously
edited edition of the *Astro-Meteorologica*.
It was a labour of love by Edward Waple, Archdeacon
of Taunton and vicar of St Sepulchre's, a well-known
Anglican clergyman, who had been taught by the Catholic Goad,
as one of his first pupils at Merchant Taylors'.
And after his death there appeared a further tribute to his memory,
written by another former pupil, Joshua Barnes,
who was later to become Professor of Greek at Cambridge.

The nineteenth-century historian of the school, also an Anglican,
wrote sorrowfully of the treatment accorded
Goad in his later years and commented: "Nor can we deny
the Roman Communion the honour of having gotten
from us in him a very learned and pious man."

But it is Barnes, his pupil, whose valediction to this
good old man we today can re-echo:

> Go, blessed saint, enjoy that peace above,
> That candid spirit and that strifeless love,
> Which thy calm soul foretasted here below,
> And griev'd and sigh'd; that all men did not so.

Rudolf Nureyev, a colossus felled by AIDS. With Margot Fonteyn in Roland Petit's ballet 'Paradise Lost', 1967.

Photograph: Houston Rogers, courtesy of V&A Images / Theatre Museum.

Chapter 9

Jesus said: Of course I want you to be cured.

Leprosy was the most feared sickness in the ancient world.
It was feared because it was contagious
and because sufferers knew they were doomed to a living hell
before death came as a merciful relief.
It was so dangerous that the laws of the time were blunt and cruel.
Once leprosy was identified, the sufferer had to leave the town
and go beyond the walls and yell out a warning
if people came too near. Unclean! Unclean!
Can you imagine the mental anguish of such outcasts –
suffering physically of course
but forced to endure heartbreak as well.
Leprosy was a great challenge to Christian love.
Jesus, of course, had the perfect solution.
He could use his divine power to eradicate the leprosy.
And on occasion did so.
But what of his followers? They had rather limited power
as miracle-workers. How could they meet the challenge?
I suppose the most celebrated fighter against leprosy was the
Belgian missionary, Fr Damien. He chose to work among lepers,
teaching them, consoling them. And when in due course
the infection reached him too, he stood at Mass one Sunday
to preach and began: "We lepers . . . "
He no longer needed to imagine their suffering from outside,
he now shared their anguish from within.
And that is deeply Christian.
All through the histories of the saints we meet priests dying
after bringing Communion to plague victims; doctors and
nurses who themselves caught typhoid, and died in effect
as martyrs of the caring vocation.

In a month which has seen a single doctor horrifying
the nation because he brought death to many of his patients,
we would do well to recall the many doctors and nurses
and surgeons who have brought life to their patients
at a fatal cost to themselves.

In our time there has been a new leprosy, an epidemic that
brought fear to its victims and forced others to shun them.
The contagious and debilitating and murderous outbreak
of AIDS. A new plague, made more horrible because it
seemed to arrive concealed under a cloak of liberty and love.
Not all liberty is genuine freedom; not all love is wise
and selfless love. Very often, those who became the victims
of this new scourge were young and beautiful and idealistic.
They did not choose AIDS; they were caught up in a delusion.
And that, I am quite sure, is how Jesus would have seen them,
as victims of delusion.

There have, alas, been many times when a disease has been
identified as a judgment of God. Job's so-called comforters
pretended sympathy, but made it clear that they thought Job
had brought his misfortunes on himself.
People are only too willing to believe that plagues are
God's revenge on sinners. But it is a repellent belief –
a belief deeply insulting to the goodness of God.
Sickness is not a curse by God. Handicaps are not God's handiwork.
Malfunctions of nature are not the will of God.
What is really sick is to suggest that illness is somehow
a judgment of the Almighty.

Lepers do not deserve to be lepers any more than lepers *choose*
to be lepers. It is appalling to make some sort of adverse
moral judgment on someone simply because they suffer.
Jesus did not say "Well, you must have brought that on yourself,"
he simply said "of course I want you to be cured."
Our duty is not to judge, but to care.

The leprosy of the twentieth century was AIDS and it has been
fatally easy for some people to blame the victims themselves.
Of course, it may well be that if they had made better choices,
they would not have fallen victim to AIDS.
Who can say? There were undoubtedly mistakes.
Indulgence in smoking may well have caused the lung cancer.
Indulgence is so-called liberated sex may well have caused AIDS.
Indulgence in alcohol may well have caused the crippling car crash.
That's beside the point.
The time when people are suffering is not the time to be making
moral judgments. It's the time for love and care,
and imagination, and understanding.

Over the last decade I have lost several friends to AIDS.
There has been much sorrow, much pain, much wastage
of bright young lives, and I often wish they had made
other choices. But again and again I have been
deeply moved by the courage of the victims and the
tremendous love of their friends. What would have been
merely a sordid tragedy of wasted life has frequently
been an inspiration, a triumph of the human spirit
over adversity and a demonstration of love
that is hard to parallel in other contexts.

People did not choose to be lepers. It simply happened.
Their leprosy was not an adverse judgment on them but
a challenge to Christians to love them in their hour of need.
People do not choose to be gay. It simply happens.
Their sexuality is not an adverse judgment on them,
but a challenge to the rest of us to help them find love.

We are perhaps fortunate to have a clear code of conduct.
And we'd be even more fortunate if we followed it ourselves.
And we'd be most fortunate of all if we met the lepers
of our own times not with blame but with love.

Statue in the Lady Chapel, Most Sacred Heart, Ruislip.

Chapter 10

All generations will call me blessed.

Today is a feast which invites us to consider
the place of Woman in our faith.
When non-Catholics look at the Church
and see our cult of the Virgin Mary
it can seem like a sort of Christian 'extra'; a rather childlike,
or even childish, devotion to a female icon.

I've heard Our Lady referred to as the Catholic Church's
saving grace.
Ours is such a religion of paternalism, male dominance,
that it needs this extra ingredient of feminine wisdom.
There's something to be said for that view.
We do use language of Father and Son.
We do have a male priesthood
that represents sacramentally God the Son.
We do have a real need to recognise
that women are increasingly wondering
how to make their presence felt in the Church.
It's all part of an on-going exploration
of the nature of the Church.

Certain things do need to be remembered.
Our transcendent God is both paternal and maternal.
The five books of the Pentateuch: Genesis, Exodus, Leviticus,
Numbers and Deuteronomy, tend to refer to the Creator
as Lord and Father.
But the Wisdom literature: Job, Proverbs, Ecclesiasticus,
Ecclesiastes and the Wisdom of Solomon produces
a different emphasis.
Although most of the Fathers use 'Wisdom' as a synonym
for the Word, the Logos, the second person of the Trinity,

there were others, like Irenaeus and Theophilus of Antioch
who equate 'Wisdom' with the Holy Spirit,
the *third* person of the Trinity.
In the Wisdom of Solomon, Wisdom appears as female
and you don't have to be a feminist to appreciate
the scriptural expressions of love for Wisdom, the Holy Spirit:

> Wisdom I loved; I sought her out when I was young
> and longed to win her for my bride;
> I fell in love with her beauty . . .
> She is initiated into the knowledge that belongs to God
> and she decides for him what he shall do . . .
> temperance and prudence, justice and fortitude,
> these are her teachings . . .
> So I determined to bring her home to live with me,
> knowing that she would be my counsellor in prosperity
> and my comfort in anxiety and grief.
> Through her, I shall have immortality . . .

There is plenty in our faith, even in the Hebrew Testament,
to make us aware of the feminine in God,
in God's own nature and in God's creation.

So, in that sense, Mary the Mother of God,
came into a spiritual climate which was not hostile to her.
She's not just the token woman in a man's universe.
She takes her place very gently in the scriptures:
the maiden who accepts her call from God to become
the Mother of his Son,
the kindly pregnant girl who walks up to the hills
to lend practical support to the much older Elizabeth,
the observant wedding guest who propelled her divine Son
into his first revelation of miraculous power,
the undeterred Mother, standing courageously
at the foot of the Cross,
the companion of her son's apostles in the Upper Room:
Mary, the Queen Mother of Christianity,

safe in the keeping of John, the disciple Jesus loved.
Mary isn't an optional extra: she's mainstream.

And as the second Christian millennium went on
Mary's role came ever more sharply into focus.
Her role as Mother to God's Son needed the preparation
of her Immaculate Conception.
And when her earthly lifespan finally came to an end,
the total sinlessness of her life meant that
when she went to sleep she was assumed instantaneously
into the eternal presence of her Creator and her Son.

So essential is her role that the great Jesuit,
Gerard Manley Hopkins, compared her to the air we breathe.
Every breath we take reminds him:

> Of her who not only
> Gave God's infinity
> (Dwindled to infancy)
> Welcome in womb and breast.
> Birth, milk, and all the rest,
> But mothers each new grace
> That does now reach our race –
> Mary Immaculate,
> Merely a women, yet
> Whose presence, power is
> Great as no goddess's
> Was deemèd, dreamèd who
> This one work has to do –
> Let all God's glory through.

It is literally a breathtaking vision of the significance of Mary.

Her great task is always to bring us closer to Jesus,
to point us towards Jesus, to draw us to him,
to explain him to us, to mediate between her divine Son
and all of us who are by adoption his siblings.

Through her we may see him
Made sweeter, not made dim.
And her hand leaves his light
Sifted to suit our sight.

It is the air we breathe which sustains our life
and in the same way it is the influence of Mary
which sustains our spiritual life.
She is a gentle humanising channel of the grace of God.

Just as trees filter the strong sunshine,
so the hand of Mary softens the justice of God.
The brightness of His glory would blind us;
she softens its brightness to suit our human sight.
Like her Son, she helps us to grasp
the sheer depth of love in the heart of God.

The old emphasis on God, "the god of old",
as a figure of anger and revenge and destruction,
was transfigured by Mary and her Son.
It was the coming into history of the holy family,
the Virgin Mother, her protective husband Joseph,
and her divine Son, which enabled us
to appreciate a different aspect of God.

When Mary is the air we breathe,
we speak prayers, not of fear but love:

    Stir in my ears, speak there
    Of God's love, O live air,
    Of patience, penance, prayer:
    World-mothering air, air wild,
    Wound with thee, in thee isled
    Fold home, fast fold thy child.

In man's first awareness of God, it was the male strengths,
the masculine virtues which dominated mankind's perception.
In the later insights of the Wisdom literature

different strengths and virtues were perceived –
insight and wisdom,
and we saw Wisdom eulogised as the Holy Spirit.
And when that male/female balance was achieved,
the time was ripe
for bringing into the awareness of the world
a Saviour who was Christ the Lord,
a God-made-man
whose human nature depended
on the womb of a perfect woman.

Christianity has been blessed with many insights
and few of them have altered the climate of our spiritual lives
more than the deepening devotion to Our Blessed Lady.

All generation have called her blessed
and she has indeed become to us the very air we breathe.

The Infant of Prague, the divine child
robed and crowned as a king.

Chapter 11

The Lord is King, with majesty enrobed

I first knew Jesus of Nazareth when he was a tiny baby.
I remember the beautiful grotto in the side aisle
of Holy Rood in Watford which housed the Christmas Crib.
Real straw!
And a sense of profound peace and goodness
centred on the baby in swaddling clothes,
lying in the manger.
It appealed to me all those years ago and I hope
other children this Christmas will experience baby Jesus
in such an appealing way.
It's the first step towards understanding
the fullness of God's love
to understand that the creator of the universe
became a helpless human baby.
Later on, at First Communion time, we sang a hymn:

> Little King so fair and sweet,
> See us gathered round thy feet . . .
> Be thou Monarch of our school,
> It shall prosper 'neath thy rule.
> We will be thy subjects true,
> Brave to suffer, brave to do,
> All our hearts to thee we bring.
> Take them, keep them little King.

Later on still, I thought that maybe that was all a bit childish
and was almost embarrassed by it, until I realised
that children see things in a way that adults simply fail to see.
That picture of the Little King Jesus was, in fact,
innocent and lovely.

It was beautifully portrayed in the statue of
the Infant of Prague.

It's a statue of the young boy Jesus,
venerated in one of the churches in Prague,
and dressed in the amazing embroidered robes
and elaborate crown of a baroque king.
It was oddly moving to see a child dolled up in such grandeur.
A powerful image loved all over the world.

So when I accompanied the BBC Symphony Orchestra
on a visit to Prague in the eighties I wanted to see it
for myself – but the authorities were very reluctant.
It was too far to walk, the church was closed for redecoration.
There were more significant things to see.
I had to insist and they were very cross with me.
Imagine a Communist regime feeling itself threatened
by a statue of a little boy togged up as an earthly king.
But they were right to feel threatened.
The Communist regime has fallen.
The Infant of Prague remains, and I was delighted recently
when a young parishioner brought me a miniature
representation of it.

The Little Lord is king, with majesty enrobed.
The Little Lord Jesus, asleep on the hay.

And then I began to understand other images.
Alongside the vision of sovereignty, kingly power and glory,
there is a contrasting image of a prisoner who stands
before the Roman Governor, Pontius Pilate.
It is suggested that this abused prisoner is a king,
'The King of the Jews'.
Instead of a crown of gold,
flashing fire from its multitude of jewels,

there is a crown made of thorns,
a crown that is both a mockery of kings
and the epitome of kingship.
Kingship as the pinnacle of love.
"My kingdom", said Jesus, "is not of this world."
"You *are* a king then?" replied Pilate.
"Yes, I am," said Jesus. "I was born for this."
And the wheel turns full circle: the all-powerful wields power
through having relinquished power.

The King of Calvary is the baby in the manger.
If you want a profound meditation
on the Incarnation this Christmas
read Oscar Wilde's short story, *The Selfish Giant*.
The child who brings spring to a winter garden
is the Lord of Life,
and he is Lord of Life because
he sacrificed life and went through death
and rose to life again.

St Robert Southwell's image of the Burning Babe of Bethlehem.
The image of the Infant of Prague.
The image of the prisoner crowned with thorns.
The child defeating winter in the Giant's garden.
All these deepen our awareness of who Jesus is.

Today is the feast of Christ the King.
I treasure the words of Thérèse of Lisieux,
St Thérèse of the Child Jesus.
She looked at him appearing before her all radiant with love.

> O Jesus, my little brother,
> I want no other joy than that of pleasing you.
> O my little King, give me the virtues of your childhood.

Chapter 12

Help us to express in our lives the love we celebrate.

The only time I ever saw Grace Kelly myself was when she'd
become Princess Grace and was introducing a Sinatra concert
at the Royal Festival Hall and I remember her remarking that
nearly everyone had their own particular Sinatra favourite –
and it was different from everyone else's.
I knew what she meant. He wasn't a one-song guy.
No other singer has covered so many aspects of human love –
from high hopes to the blues, from *Blue Skies* to
Stormy Weather.
If you were to make a study of the lyrics of all the songs
Sinatra recorded you'd have a tremendous insight
into all the complexities of the human heart.
The lyrical simplicity of *Little One* from *High Society,*
the world-weary depression of *One for the Road.*
For myself I'll say prayers for his eternal rest
out of sheer gratitude for the recording he made
of Tchaikovsky's *None but the lonely heart.*
Sad that such a talent went along with such a complicated
private life. You can't but be sad to read alongside the
musical successes of Sinatra's career the miserable
consequences of the wealth they brought him.
One paper said he'd died heartbroken because his wife
and his children were at loggerheads over his estate.
The words of one of his greatest hits seem like
a slap in the face: *Who wants to be a millionaire?*

Last Wednesday I heard news of the death of another
eighty year-old, much closer to home.
Sister St James was a good pal for many years.
She was one of the Filles de Jésus – the nuns

who built the convent and founded the school
dedicated to St Joan of Arc in Rickmansworth.
She was a very bright, brisk, businesslike woman,
full of energy and high spirits.
She was a good teacher and she had a real-life sister,
also a nun, also at Joan of Arc, who played the organ
in Ricky church and sang in a voice I can still hear
from my childhood – a voice that had the richness
of timbre of a Kathleen Ferrier.

Sister St James eventually became headmistress of
St Joan of Arc – I think she may have been the last nun
to hold that job. And when she retired from that,
she became Provincial of the Order.
She gave me enormous encouragement in my priesthood,
understanding the stresses and strains and urging
good sense all the time. She's been here several times.
And – more important to me even than that –
she always kept an eye on my mother.

In her eighties Mother frequently went down to daily Mass
in Ricky and the nuns from Nightingale Road would often
ask her in for a cuppa after. And when, past ninety,
Mother became unable to go out, Sister St James was
one of her most faithful visitors.
They were both teachers and Sister St James understood
the frustrations about which my mother never complained.
She moved down to a convent in Kent but even then,
whenever she paid a visit to Ricky, she'd try to call in
on my mother.

Early on Tuesday morning, the other nun in the house
heard a small commotion. Sister St James said, very firmly:
"Sister, you'd better call a doctor. I'm dying."
And she sat in an armchair and died.

A sudden, but not an unprovided death. At eighty, she was
perfectly prepared. She had no money to leave anyone, but she has
left many hearts full of gratitude for all she gave
to her vocation as a teacher, as a Head, as a religious.

As it so happened, the next Mass I was booked to say
after hearing the news of her death
was the voluntary weekly early-morning Mass in the
little Chapel of St Joan of Arc School on Thursday morning.
It was a deep joy to be able to say Mass for the repose of her soul
in the school where she had taught and I had learned.

I've been thinking so much of these two lives, now ended:
Frank Sinatra. Sister St James.
God gave them both such gifts and they reaped many rewards.
Sinatra was able to claim with some truth 'I did it my way' –
and had his fame and his wealth but in his last days
his heart was troubled.
Sister had long given up trying to do anything her way;
she lived her life trying to discover what was God's way
and she died as she had lived, quickly, efficiently and happily.

I pray for them both. I thank God for them both.
They lived their different lives heart and soul.
And though the one ended with wealth and fame,
it's the other I really envy.
She had the deep happiness of being able to look back
over a long life of giving to others.
The best I can do with my life is not to do it my way,
but to hand it to God and try to do it His way.

Chapter 13

Her sins, her many sins, must have been forgiven her
or she would not have shown such great love.

The greatest sin is betrayal.
It's when someone bites the hand that feeds him.
It's when I promise love and fail to deliver.
It's when I say Trust me, and betray that trust.
There's nothing more destructive of human relationships
than betrayal.
And we do our best to dress it up in more respectable guises:
"He told me in confidence, but of course
honesty compels me . . . "
"I promised I would come but it was very unwise
to have made the promise . . . "
"Love was simply too strong for me;
I know I had promised fidelity, but when this other woman came
along I knew it was right for me . . . "
All the excuses in the world to pretend
that there was no betrayal.
Such excuses butter no parsnips.
Betrayal is ignominious.
Treachery is the correct name for adultery.
Treason is a capital offence.

Take the case of David.
He'd been handpicked by the prophet Samuel
to replace Saul as King.
He was given the crown by divine command.
And in many ways he was a good king.
But then self-delusion entered David's life.
He was smitten by a married woman
and deliberately sent the husband into battle
hoping he would be killed. And he was.

And David took the woman. Lousy behaviour.
Betrayal of one of his own soldiers.
Betrayal of his high office.
Betrayal of God.
Behaviour that justified God's anger.

The one redeeming fact is that when David realised
what he had persuaded himself to do
he was overcome with shame and repented bitterly.
It's not a nice experience to look in the mirror
and see a gross sinner.

And it was the same with the woman who anointed Christ.
When she looked in the mirror she saw the beautiful features
which enabled her to flourish in the oldest profession
and it gave her no joy to see her beauty because
she knew that the treacherous men who bought her services
had no regard for her as a person.
She was just an object of lust.

The beauty she saw in the mirror was compromised
by its abuse and it wasn't until Jesus came along
and valued her for herself and called her out of that life
that she could look in the mirror and enjoy what she saw.
Beautiful but abused, valued but betrayed,
no wonder she should find in Jesus the start of a new life.

Her gratitude to him was overwhelming
and she did not hold back from showing it.
Pouring precious ointment over the feet of Christ,
washing them with her tears, wiping them with her hair –
extravagant gestures from an extravagant woman,
but – as he was the first to recognise – dead genuine.

Her way of life had been a way of death.
But he cast out her demons and she became
one of his closest followers.

For this reason, her sins were forgiven.
Her world of betrayals melted into trust of God.
He was ready to forgive her sins, her many sins,
and to open up the way to love.

What is the opposite of love?
Some would say hatred,
but hatred generally keeps its distance.
The real opposite of love is betrayal.
To love is to trust someone and to be trustworthy for them.
Betrayal is the destruction of love
and is the greatest of all sins, the sin against trust.
The sin of Judas was not that he hated Christ,
but that he betrayed him.

We can understand the exaggerated devotion
of the former sinner when we remember
how often she had betrayed her best self
and been betrayed by many men.
Her extravagant gestures of love are the response
of someone whose ability to trust has been restored.

Two characters. A king and a prostitute.
Both ensnared in betrayal. Both desperately ashamed.
Both overwhelmed by God's willingness to forgive.
Their stories fill me with hope.
Hope that my own awareness of my sins,
my many sins, may bring me to a similar awareness
of that overwhelming forgiveness
and enable me to respond as they did
with new lives
showing the influence of such great love.

There is a moment in every Mass when we not only speak of making peace but make our goodwill visible. At the Mass at Our Lady of Hal in Camden Town at which I was ordained deacon, the sign of peace became an emotional moment for my mother. Next to her my sister Deirdre, and in the foreground Bishop Kenneth Woollcombe.

Chapter 14

In every place then, I want the men to lift up their hands
reverently in prayer with no anger or argument.

One of the most remarkable features
of this Church of St William of York
is that it contains a clock,
and not just a clock, but a striking clock.
Every half hour it marks the passage of time.
There are a few churches with clocks
– but usually silent ones.
Sacred Heart in Ruislip had one on the front of the gallery
which was useful when I was preaching.
What's so absolutely amazing about our clock
here in Stanmore is that it's not where *I* can see it
but where *you* can see it!
What reckless courage to put a clock
right behind the preacher's head,
so the people can keep tabs on the length of the sermon
as it's happening!

It reminded me of a clock brought into the cathedral
in Florence by the architect Brunelleschi
while he was building the great Dome.
The workmen coming in to work had to sign on
– and then they were reminded of the time worked
throughout the day by this clock which struck
every half-hour.

That was the period when they were sorting out time.
Until the fifteenth century the key word was *hora*.
Hora meant an hour but it was the same word
as *ora* meaning prayer.

And the hours of the day were just that – times for prayer:
following the discipline of the monks who got up in the dark
to pray, and then prayed at *regular hours* through the day –
the hours for prayer: Matins and Lauds, Prime, Terce,
Sext, None, Vespers and Compline.

That daily sequence of prayer sessions became distilled
into books known as the Divine Office.
Monks and nuns sang or said the office.
The portrait of Cardinal Basil Hume
in the National Portrait Gallery shows him sitting quietly
with his breviary, saying his office.
A powerful image, indicating priorities.

Interestingly, one of the small reforms of Vatican II
was to leave aside the old phrase Divine Office
and call it The Liturgy of the Hours.
It's a good reminder of the close relationship
of the words *hora* and *ora:* hour and prayer.

Before Brunelleschi's time the hours were subdivided
into shorter sections and very short moments.
It was only at the Renaissance that hours were divided
into sixty minutes and minutes into secondary sixtieths.
And as those more structured hours came into universal use
so did a wonderful variety of prayer books
which were known as Primers or Books of Hours,
designed to foster the prayer-life of ordinary people
who didn't have the time to observe a full monastic
regime of prayer.
To begin with they were luxury items,
gorgeously illuminated and gilded, and hand-written,
so only the very rich could afford them.
But the coming of the printing press
made them much more accessible.

When William Caxton set up his press at Westminster Abbey
in 1476 he produced the first liturgical book
printed in this country: a Primer, a Book of Hours.

Why am I telling you this?
Because I'm sure that at this time of heightened tension
in the world we need to pray a lot more, to think prayerfully,
to read prayerfully and simply to be at peace prayerfully.

We all need to be closer to God, able to listen to God.
It ought to be our constant concern to bring our minds
back from anger and fear and the general muddle of our lives
to the clarity of God's purpose:
fulfilment and freedom and friendship.

During World War Two, people gathered round the wireless
every evening to listen to the News at nine o'clock,
and as Big Ben led up to nine o'clock and the nine strokes
rang out from Westminster, people prayed
in the silence of their hearts for peace.
If you have in your house a striking clock
let each hour that strikes be a cue for prayer.
When the clock strikes in church, pray for peace.
Find every excuse and prompt and reminder to pray for peace.
That sort of prayer is desperately needed.

Hour and Prayer. *Hora et ora.*
Let them be connected in our lives
and not only will our prayers increase, but we will become
more recollected, more tranquil, more serene.
Monks and nuns regulate their work by the convent bell,
a clear call to prayer.
From the minaret of the mosque the faithful of Islam
are called to prayer.
And we must respond to that imperative to pray
– to put God first, to put Love at the top of the agenda,
to create peace in our hearts.

Keep an ear on the clock, and on the hour turn aside to pray.
Even the irritating bleep of a digital watch
can be a reminder to pray.
Use other signals too.
When a telephone rings or a police-car wails,
when a tannoy blares or a dog barks,
when a record comes to an end – pray.

I use the sound of applause at the end of a concert
or in a theatre as a prompt to encourage me to thank God.
I use the Greenwich Time Signal to make the sign of the cross
and pray in my heart for peace. It's necessary.

As Paul wrote to Timothy two thousand years ago,
"My advice is that first of all there should be prayer
offered for everyone
– petitions, intercessions and thanksgiving
– and especially for kings and others in authority
so that we may be able to live religious and reverent lives
in peace and quiet."
Amen. Amen.

Chapter 15

God does not have favourites, . . . anybody
of any nationality who fears God and does
what is right is acceptable to him.

That statement by the first Bishop of Rome
is clearly a manifesto for tolerance.
It breaks decisively with the notion
that there is a chosen people,
defined racially or ethnically.

The people of God is the whole of humanity
– and within that all-embracing category,
God is particularly likely to support
the oppressed and the poor.

Which explains why God came to the rescue of the Israelites
when they were prisoners in Egypt.
God was on their side against those who oppressed them
– and the spiritual strength he gave them
empowered them to escape.
What happened subsequently was
that those whom God trained, and strengthened, and led,
did indeed escape – and then reached the point
of worldly prosperity where they didn't need him any more.
They turned away from him then
and worshipped a golden calf instead.

And that, I'm afraid, is a summary of an often-repeated
sequence of events.
In starving Ireland, God gave the strength
which bound the people together in resistance
to the predatory power of the landlords
– but the more prosperous Ireland becomes,
the more God is regarded as superfluous.

In occupied and Soviet-controlled Poland,
God inspired the spiritual strength which gives solidarity
to the people – but once the struggle for freedom is won,
Mammon takes over.

It's a saga many times repeated.
But it should not surprise us.
Difficulty – adversity – is what brings out the best in people
whereas when we're only coasting along,
it's easy to forget God.

The one thing you can safely predict about people
who fall away from love is their ingratitude.
So we have to remind ourselves that
although we follow the Christ who is the Way,
the Truth and the Life – and although we are members
of the one Holy Catholic and Apostolic Church,
that status in itself is not enough to save us.
Indeed it is more than likely that it will lull us
into a false sense of security and encourage us
to assume that because we belong to God's chosen,
we needn't *bother* with God any more!

Oh come off it, Father! That doesn't really happen.
Can you really see that happening in Middlesex
in the diocese of Westminster, *now*?
Certainly I can.

Ask yourself this question:
How many Catholic people who promise God
they'll be his faithful followers
are doing so in order to escape – they and their children –
to escape from the perceived inadequacies of state schools?
And as soon as their children have bagged a place
in a Catholic school, their gratitude to God evaporates
and they slide away from practice.
Their religion is merely token.
They go to Mass until their earthly ambition is achieved

and then they gradually fall away.
They still wear a Catholic label but the deed
which defines a Catholic – coming to Mass every Sunday –
falls out of their busy schedule.
Of course they don't have time for it.
Time to watch twenty hours of television a week,
Time to go to aerobics classes,
Time to wash the cars,
Time to relax in the pub,
But no time for Mass.

The ingratitude is as obvious here and now
as it was in the time of Moses.
The ungrateful are apt to defend their behaviour by saying:
well – it doesn't really matter does it.
And they parody the words of St Peter – as long as you
believe in God and lead a good life, that's all you need.
And thus do they defend a self-centred lifestyle
in which they pretend to be aware of God
and permit all their selfishness to masquerade as the good life.

God is not mocked.
He requires more than an occasional wave.
He expects more than consumer greed
wrapped up as 'decent standards'.
His very first commandment calls us to believe in God,
to hope in him, "and to love him *above everything else*."
Only if we can honestly say we live like that
can we be doing what is right.

You can't love someone you don't know
and to imagine that a nodding acquaintance with God
is loving him above everything else
is the most pathetic of delusions.
St Peter rightly warned against the complacency
of believing that because you wear a particular label
you are *in*.

Anybody, of any nationality, who fears God
and *does* what is right, is acceptable to God.
That's the requirement and it gives no comfort
to those who imagine
they can get away with token gestures and lip service.

Parents who are cynical and ungrateful
will generate their own particular hell:
cynical and ungrateful children.

As the people of Moses discovered long ago,
those who fall away from God
and live ungratefully and love minimally
can only expect to reap what they sow.
Thin sowing; thin reaping.

Chapter 16

Zeal for your house will devour me.

The largest of the Oxford Colleges was originally
launched in 1525 by Cardinal Wolsey.
When he fell from power everything he had
was confiscated by King Henry VIII
who disliked the name Cardinal College
and re-christened it King Henry VIII College.
But that didn't last long either.
The King himself suppressed it and when he started up
a new diocese of Oxford, gave the college building
to the new bishop as his Cathedral.
To this day it is the only Oxbridge college
which has a cathedral as its chapel.

And it was given a new name: Christ Church.
Its Latin name is slightly different: *Aedes Christi.*
Aedes. The word could mean a temple
but its main meaning is a dwelling, a house.
We see it in the English word edifice
– a constructed dwelling.
So Aedes Christi is not so much the Church of Christ
but a *House* of Christ and that is why, to this day,
the Students and undergraduates of Christ Church
refer to their college affectionately, not as Christ Church,
but as The House.
It's a very imposing college and the buildings,
including the cathedral,
house an academic community dedicated to study.
In this way, the Aedes Christi, the House of Christ,
enshrines the spirit of Christ.
It makes visible a regime of study and an ideal
of learning for a spiritual reason.

Down through the ages men and women
have tried to create buildings where they hope
God may feel at home: temples, cathedrals, shrines,
oratories, hermitages, buildings both large and small,
which man can dedicate to God and beg God to inhabit.
The buildings themselves are important,
but even more important are the realities within.
The true and deep meaning of a college is not its stones,
not its libraries, nor even its chapel, but its community
of students, its collegiate identity, its very soul.
By the same token, the true and deep meaning of a church
is not its bricks, not its statues, not even its altars,
but its presence of Christ, its reason for being, its very soul.
And it is that deeper meaning which demands zeal from us,
zeal for thy house.
We show zeal for God's house, not because it is
the most lovely work of our hands,
but because it is *Aedes Christi*, the house of Christ.

You see that same essential truth made plain
in negative ways too.
On Thursday night the allied air forces targeted bombs
on the presidential palaces of Saddam Hussein.
Why? They knew that he and his henchmen
would almost certainly not be there and that only janitors
and cleaners would be around at midnight.
But those palaces had been erected to represent
the dominance and power of a regime.
They were not only operations centres but symbols
of the durability of tyranny.
So the destruction of the presidential palaces
became just as symbolic as the destruction of the twin towers,
or the sack of Rome, or the fall of the Bastille,
or the blowing up of Nelson's pillar in Dublin.

What we have to do is to understand

what goes on behind the symbols:
we have to go to the reality beyond, to the human beings
who live the lives the buildings represent.
The bombers may have reduced the buildings to rubble
– but what of the people who animated those buildings?
If they have identified themselves with the purpose
of those buildings, tyranny will survive.
But if they can free themselves from their slavery
to what those buildings express, there is hope.

It's very hard this weekend not to think about
those blitzed palaces and to hope and pray
that the tyranny they express can also be destroyed.
But what then can we build in their place?

We feel pretty helpless now about the course of the war itself,
but what follows is very dependent on us.
The building we need is one in which the animating spirit
is love: a house of God, a church, a Christ Church
that is a *genuine* house of Christ.

What we have to remember is that *we* are
both the bricks and mortar
and the animating spirit of the house of Christ.

There are many in Iraq, and many in our own country,
who if we are not careful will see our churches,
our houses of Christ, as the presidential palaces
of a Christian tyranny, driven by power and greed.
And we have to demonstrate in our lives
that our houses of Christ are full of love
and understanding and compassion.
Our zeal for the house of God springs from our reverence
for the *love* of God.
Those who come regularly to the house of God
must prove that they are filled
with love of God and all his children.

Pope John Paul II celebrates Mass al fresco outside Mary's house on 30 November 1979. Photograph courtesy of Veritas Books.

Chapter 17

I will not leave you orphans.

Who did Jesus love more than anyone else?
His mother, of course. Mary.
We know he was a man with a great heart.
He enjoyed many friendships, not least with Martha,
Mary and Lazarus – and he had one friend so close
that he is referred to as 'the beloved disciple'.
When Jesus was hanging on the cross, dying,
he turned to that loved friend, John, to make his last request.
John recorded it in his Gospel:

> When Jesus therefore saw his mother and the disciple
> standing by, whom he loved, he said to his Mother
> 'Woman behold thy son'.
> Then he said to the disciple: 'Behold thy Mother'.
> And from that hour the disciple took her into his home.

For a time she stayed in Jerusalem, among the apostles.
As St Luke describes it in the Acts,
the apostles were constantly at prayer together
and with them a group of women, including
Mary the Mother of Jesus.
And that is the last we hear of Mary in the Bible.

After Pentecost the increasing number of converts
met constantly to hear the apostles teach
and to share the common life, to break bread and to pray.
John and Peter were the main leaders
and John kept his promise to look after Mother Mary.
For a time things looked safe enough but round about 37 AD
the Pharisees once more took up the cudgels
against the followers of Jesus,

and a persecution was launched in Jerusalem which resulted
in the charismatic deacon Stephen being stoned to death.
A new Herod came to the throne and ordered the arrest
of Peter and then beheaded James, the brother of John.
John decided to get out, and to take Mary with him into exile.
Years before, she had been taken to safety in Egypt,
by Joseph, to escape the massacre of babies
ordered by the earlier Herod.
Now she had to become a refugee again,
leaving everything behind her.
All those years ago she had been a young mother,
healthy and strong.
This time she was a widow, probably in her fifties,
being protected by her dead son's best friend.

John decided they would go to Ephesus,
a huge city of a quarter of a million people
on the coast of what today is Turkey.
It was that flourishing city which was to be the springboard
for the first great wave of Christian preaching.
Paul and John both spent some years in Ephesus.
It may well have been there that John began
to jot down his Gospel.
It was a pagan city containing one of the wonders
of the ancient world, the colossal marble
Temple of Artemis, the Mother Goddess.
And it was prosperous, with good water supplies
and public baths, even street lighting at night
– a luxury shared only by Rome and Antioch.
Mary settled there, happily enough, not wanting to take
a prominent role – content to be looked after by John.
For a few months she lived in the city itself,
in a house rented by John. But he wanted to settle her
somewhere quieter, more secluded, out of the way.

He bought land on Nightingale Mountain up above the city
and had a little house built for her up there.
Whenever Christian teachers came through Ephesus,
it's likely that they'd call to see her.
St Luke is known to have been there: it seems very likely
that he met Mary and heard first-hand from her the story
of the birth of Jesus which he tells in his Gospel.
Peter came through, accompanied as usual by Mark.

Mary stayed serenely in her little house among the nightingales
– the Queen Mother of Christianity.
John kept his promise to care for her
until she finally went to sleep.
We don't know when, precisely,
but probably before the late sixties when Paul
and then Peter were put to death in Rome.

Much later, in the eighteenth century,
Pope Benedict XIV said "the Blessed Virgin Mary
left this life in Ephesus and ascended into heaven."
Later ages called it the Dormition of the Blessed Virgin
– she simply went to sleep.
It is a lovely imaginative story.
Peter came to bring her Communion.
And when she breathed her last they noted
it was the ninth hour – just like her son.
Further up the mountain was the cave
she had chosen as her grave. They carried the body
to it with great tenderness and reverence.
Not for the first time, Thomas was missing, and when
he arrived, John took him to see the Virgin one last time.
Inside the cave, they knelt in prayer
and John slipped off the coffin lid.
Mary's body was not in the shroud but the shroud was intact.
Thomas and John carefully replaced the lid and
came wonderingly away.

The years passed, and as the harbour of Ephesus silted up,
the city went into severe economic decline.
Eventually the Christians in Ephesus
built the first church dedicated to the saint
who had come to live and die among them.

In AD 431 the third Ecumenical Council of the Church
was summoned to meet at Ephesus,
"the place where John the theologian and
the Blessed Virgin Mary, Mother of God, were."
And in the church dedicated to their beloved granny figure,
the assembled Fathers saluted the divinity of Jesus Christ
by calling his mother Theotokos, Mother of God.
Soon after, the city with all its wealth of marble
began to crumble and decay, virtually disappearing
under sand and weeds until the nineteenth century.

On the Feast of Candlemas 1960, Pope John XXIII
sent a special candle to Mary's house at Ephesus.
In 1967 Pope Paul VI visited the house,
and in 1979 Pope John Paul II said Mass
in the open air just outside Mary's house.

Marble cities crumble and fall but the little house
built by the beloved disciple still stands: to remind us
that John was given a Mother, that *we* were not left orphans –
we were given a Mother, our own Queen Mother,
Mary the Refugee, Mary the Mother of God.

Much of the material in this sermon comes from Donald Carroll:
Mary's House, *Veritas Books, London, 2000.*

Chapter 18

Why does your master eat with tax collectors?

At the time of Jesus, tax collectors had a real image problem.
We grumble a lot today about tax levels
but we generally accept that our taxes are a necessity
if we're to have our welfare state and our schools
– and we tend to think of the tax man as a necessary cog
in the wheels of civilised society.
But at the time of Jesus that wasn't the view at all.
Tax collectors then were predatory opportunists,
keeping in with the authorities by milking their neighbours
and dobbing on them if necessary.
The Roman Empire paid its bills
by taxing the provinces defended by its armies.
And taxes were paid through local agents –
collaborators with the Roman occupation forces,
who made a living out of their percentage,
the money that stuck to their fingers on its way back to Rome.
These unpopular taxmen were seen in the same lurid light
as the agents of English landlords in Ireland.
The agents were local men who knew the local people
and were prepared to earn their keep by squeezing the tenants
to keep the landlords in affluent comfort.
In a time of shortage, or even famine, the land agents
had no mercy. It was still their job to get the money.

The most notorious of all the land agents was
Captain Boycott. So flint-faced, so relentless,
that the people could only deal with him by sending him
to Coventry, having absolutely nothing to do with him.
In 1880, the only weapon the people had to counter
the merciless greed of the landowners was to isolate
the local agent, refuse to have anything to do with him

– and their tactic brought a new word into the language.
A tax collector so treated was *boycotted* by the people
he was trying to exploit.
The people of Ireland in the nineteenth century,
like the people of Israel at the time of Jesus,
saw tax collectors as bullies and they had no time for them.
And so they were a bit miffed when Jesus
refused to boycott them. They protested.
Decent folk don't have anything to do with the likes of them.
Doesn't he know the sort of person they are?
And it's hard *not* to feel sympathy with that.
Even so, Jesus has to keep reminding us
that it's not the healthy man that needs the doctor,
it's the sick who send for him.
He didn't come to hob-nob with the respectable,
but to call sinners to repentance.
And that is our vocation too.
It's fine having congenial evenings with our fellow Catholics
– probably does no harm at all.
But our real task is to preach the Gospel to the unconverted.
No one is beyond the reach of the forgiveness of God.
It's one reason actually why I admire the young Mormons
who knock on doors so earnestly.
They don't draw the line at tax collectors and sinners.
They'll reach out to anyone, even Catholic priests!
And we need to ask ourselves how frequently
we follow their example.
It's not a literal question: I don't expect you to go home now
and send off a dinner invite to the Inland Revenue.
It's an attitude question: do you really see
that every other human being is potentially a saint –
even the very one who turns you off completely?
That's the tax collector.

Chapter 19

You are Peter.

I often wonder what the other apostles made of that pun
when Jesus first spoke about his church.
They knew Simon bar Jonah only too well.
The big fisherman whose gruff loyalty to Jesus
was often compromised by rash errors of judgment.
Nevertheless, despite all his faults and flaws,
Jesus selected him and deliberately changed his name
from Simon to Peter, the Rock.
Clearly Peter still needed a lot of protective work
by the Holy Spirit to fit him for his task.
The Acts of the Apostles show him learning
new aspects of the faith in the days before he left Jerusalem
to launch the new Christian Church,
first in Antioch and then in Rome.
The presence of Peter in Rome was crucial.

We know that of all the apostles it wasn't Peter
but John whom Jesus loved best.
We know that James was looked up to
in his dominant role among the Christians in Jerusalem.
But the Rock transplanted himself to the heart
of the Roman Empire so that he could be
at the centre of the mission of Christianity.
And he was there for a very long time.
If Jesus died about the year 33 AD, Peter was not crucified
until 67 or 69 AD. That's a long gap.
To realise how long that was, ask yourself where you were
and what were you doing thirty-five years ago.
It gives you an idea of how long Peter led the Church.
Not surprisingly, his memories of what Jesus
had said and done were enormously significant,

and when eventually the Roman Empire
had had enough of him and put him to death,
those memories were collected by young Mark
into a brief life of Jesus, a Gospel.

But what else needed to be done?
The church in Rome needed to find itself a new leader.
It's so far back that no contemporary records exist.
But just as the memories of Jesus were jotted down
in letters from Paul and in the biographies of Matthew
and Luke and in the theological insights of John,
so the tradition of a succession of the inheritors
of Peter's role was remembered and passed on.

In the second century Irenaeus of Lyons,
and in the fourth century Eusebius, were able to recall
that Peter and Paul had chosen a man called Linus
to be head of the church in Rome, his twelve years in the job
maybe even overlapping with the last years of Peter.
Quite what his functions and responsibilities were,
we don't know. But he was the first link in a chain
– and after him came Anacletus, probably a slave
of Greek origin, and after him Clement.

Some early sources rate Clement very highly.
They regard him as consecrated by Peter himself
and as a most reliable repository of the teaching
and traditions of the apostles.
The one really important thing we know about Clement
is that he wrote a letter to the Christians in Corinth
which was preserved and still exists.
It is the most significant Christian document
that wasn't eventually included in the New Testament.
As the great papal historian, John Kelly, says:
"The letter is the earliest example of the intervention,
fraternal but authoritative, of the Roman church, though
not of the pope personally, in the affairs of another church.

Widely read in Christian antiquity, it was sometimes treated
as part of the New Testament canon."
Clement's prestige was enormous and it is quite likely
that the present church of San Clemente, in Rome,
stands on the site of Clement's house.

Thus began the organic growth of the authority of Rome.
Over the centuries its bishops were acknowledged
by other churches as arbitrators, solvers of problems,
judges of disputes and appointers of bishops.
By the middle of the third century the pope called Stephen
was the first to find biblical authority for the primacy of Rome
in chapter 16 of Matthew's Gospel.
Like all the other teachings of the Church,
understanding deepened as the years passed.
The Catholic Church did not miraculously appear
as a pre-fabricated structure – it grew,
organically, shaped by events and personalities,
and by the guidance of the Holy Spirit, to become
what it now is. As Our Lord said,
"You are Peter, and on this rock, I *will* build my Church."

By 1870 the Church had realised the true solidity of the Rock,
and proclaimed that the Bishop of Rome is preserved
from error by the Holy Spirit on those occasions
when he speaks *ex cathedra*, on faith and morals.
There have been good men and bad men occupying
the throne of Peter – and honesty compels us to admit
that some of the worst villains have been
the most effective popes and some of the most holy men
have been the most useless popes.
The individual doesn't matter – it's the office itself
that is the Rock.

Cormac with Mother and Daddy. "As children we didn't lack anything, but I now realise how much perfectly legitimate pleasure she simply did without to make sure we had enough."

Chapter 20

No servant can be the slave of two masters.

So the mission is over and it's been a good couple of weeks.
The mission services were great and I got a feeling
of happy involvement in the parish.
The healing service was very moving,
the story of the Passover and the Mass was brilliant,
and Friday night – with the children bringing their flowers
to Our Lady – was delightful.

Best of all, Fr Michael has a way of saying Mass
that reminded us what a deep prayer it is.

For myself I've found the events of the last four weeks
a genuine reawakening:
my mother's death and funeral
followed immediately by the Mission.
I've been asking myself what really *is* important in my life
and how can I live my life to fit that situation.
As I looked back at my mother's long life
from the conclusion of it, I could see the essentials –
her dedication to three things:
the family, the children she taught, and the Mass.
But those three weren't in conflict with one another.
They were three different aspects of her faith.
She found the Real Presence of Jesus in the Mass
and he walked beside her as a teacher,
and alongside her too as a mother.

But there were all sorts of other things she brushed aside,
perfectly legitimate things which – as I now realise –
she decided she had no room for in her life.

She couldn't be bothered with any sort of showing off
or extravagance. She'd dress up for special occasions
and she certainly never dressed sloppily for school,
but when we were clearing her dressing table
I remembered that though she'd dab a shiny nose with talc,
she never used lipstick. She'd put cream on her face
last thing and had lovely skin even in very old age
but she never wore make-up during the day.
Probably couldn't afford it and had better things
to do with her time.

Don't get me wrong. I'm not saying that no woman
should ever put on her war paint – there's some needs
quite a lot of camouflage!
No, what I'm noticing is that she had her priorities.
When she was a flapper, she smoked.
When she became a mother, she stopped.
She looked at her life regularly and made choices.
As children we didn't lack anything, but I now realise
how much perfectly legitimate pleasure
she simply did without to make sure *we* had enough.

It's those inconspicuous choices that reveal
whether we are Christian in our hearts or not.
Day by day, we make choices:
to go to Mass or to go to football;
to forgive or to nurse a grudge;
to gossip or to keep mum.
And of all the choices we make,
the biggest are whether to be generous or not.

Generosity.
I'm not advocating selling up and giving all the proceeds
to CAFOD. That would be quixotic, foolish and melodramatic.
I'm not talking about generosity with money.

Flinging money at a problem hoping it will go away is often
only a sham generosity.
I mean generousness of heart.
Giving time and space in life to God and to neighbour.

The crude choice between God and Mammon
doesn't often happen: should I rob a bank or not?
It's much more a matter of checking the daily details.

My Mother filled every minute of her days and yet always
had time for God, for her pupils and for her family.
I think that's what our missioner has been saying.
Have time for God, have time for people.

Don't let earning a living – don't let affording the trimmings –
drive out the real priorities.

The only things worth doing are the ones where you can
clearly see Jesus alongside you as you do them.

If you can't see him there, it'll be Mammon you're with,
and in the long run Mammon is a treacherous
and unreliable friend.

The feast of the Holy Innocents so soon after Christmas is always a reminder of how vulnerable babies are. When a child is still-born or dies soon after birth, the grief is hard to bear. And our society increasingly kills babies before they can be born. The Church is overjoyed when a baby is born safely and is brought to the church for baptism. For the priest it is the joy of opening the channels of grace that will flow into this new being.

Fr Cormac baptised Thomas Howard at Most Sacred Heart Ruislip on 20 September 1998. (Thomas's twin sister Ciara was stillborn. Their birth had taken place on the same evening that Grace Rigby died.)

Chapter 21

Holy Innocents.

Christmas is a feast that very much centres
on the beginning of a life – the birth of a baby.
And Monday is the feast of the Holy Innocents,
those innocent victims of King Herod.
You remember when he heard the three wise men
who'd come to find a new-born King, he panicked
and had all the baby boys under the age of two
put to death so that no one would grow up to challenge him.
The birth of innocence; the death of innocence.

Why does it seem so dreadful to us when the good die young?
Looked at objectively, it really doesn't matter whether
someone lives ninety years on this earth or ninety minutes.
The life that has been created belongs to God
and realises its full potential with God.
The length of our earthly life is neither here nor there.
The only thing is that we should want to put our human life
at God's service to do whatever he wants us to do.

In my family we usually describe my mother as the only girl.
But that's not strictly true.
She had four brothers, Frank, Austin, Wilf and Gerald,
but we also knew that there were others sometime between herself
and the youngest brother. She told me ages ago
that her mother had lost twins very late in a pregnancy –
a girl called Kathleen and a boy called Michael Davitt.
Investigations have shown no record of the little girl –
and I assume that's because she died before birth
and in those days no formal record was made of the stillborn.
But the family has now found a birth registration
for her twin: Michael Davitt McCormack was born

and lived for ten minutes.
A real innocent.

What purpose can God possibly have for such a short lifespan?
Here on earth it's hard to understand.
But little Michael was never forgotten and perhaps
one of his purposes in God's plan was to help us today,
ninety years after his short life, to think about its significance
and the way we think of Holy Innocents like him.
The one thing we can be absolutely sure of
is that he went straight to heaven.
He had had no capacity to estrange himself from God –
he died long before he could spoil that original innocence.
Born, named, baptised, died: all in ten minutes.
And then he found himself among the saints alongside
the little sister who is very clearly recorded in God's books
even if she doesn't register in human records.
Among the saints!

So we can pray to them, to pray for us,
just as we can pray to any of the canonised saints
of the Church with absolute confidence.

Normally, when someone dies, we pray
that God will forgive them.
We know that we are all of us imperfect and will go
to Heaven only through the experience of Purgatory.
So we say prayers for the dead; we light candles to symbolise
those prayers to help them on their way.
But – and this is the significance of the Feast of the Holy Innocents
– there are beings in heaven who once
were tiny children, but who have now reached
the fulfilment of their human lives.
And because they are *now* fulfilled, they are able to respond
to our requests for help.
They are close to God – none closer –
and probably all of us have innocents *we* can call on,

to pray for us, to whisper in God's ear on our behalf.
So, I think of my long-dead aunt and uncle,
Kathleen and Michael Davitt.
I ask them to pray for me and I'm sure they do.
I can light a candle – not for them but to them,
in their honour, thanking God for their short life on earth
and their long life in eternity,
and asking them to keep an eye on me.
I'd love to have been there
when Mother went to heaven in August
and met them for the first time
in the fullness of their personhood.

It will always be a mystery why some lives are so short
and some so long, but we are too close to the canvas
to see the overall picture.
You have to be standing *right* back in eternity itself
before it becomes clear and everything falls into place.

We can only trust God that the one thing he'd never waste
is a human life.

When Monday comes and we celebrate the Feast of those
particular Innocents who were killed by Herod,
we can pray not just to them but to all the miscarried
and the stillborn and the aborted, innocents all,
and pray to them in Heaven to pray for us,
still struggling here on earth.

Chapter 22

And the Word was made flesh and dwelt among us.

When you've fallen head over heels in love,
it's so difficult to find the words to express your feelings.

Sometime pop music helps – you latch on to particular words
that go quite a long way to expressing what you feel.
You can sing along with a record and it feels O.K.
But then when you're trying to say 'I love you'
directly to the person you love, how impossible that is!

Words just won't come in an easy way:

Round in circles I go, longing to tell you
but afraid and shy,
I let my golden chances pass me by.
Soon you'll leave me,
off you will go in the mist of days
never, never to know
how I loved you, if I loved you.

The sheer inadequacy of words to match the depths of feeling!

It's a problem older than time.
Love has existed for all eternity.
Within the Trinity, God the Father has loved God the Son,
and the Son has returned that perfect love.
When God expresses his love, he speaks the Word
and that Word expresses the essence of God himself.
No one but God can fully understand that Word,
but he wants *us* to understand what it is he's saying.
He's longing for us to understand
and so the only way he can do it
is to enable the Word that he speaks
to take on a human form, take flesh, become man.

That's what we mean by the Incarnation.

God's love is inexpressible;
the human words don't exist to express it.
So the only way for him to express his secret love
is to shout it from the highest hill, the hill of Calvary.

At the first Christmas, God's Word became flesh.
God uttered the word of love and the word became flesh.
Jesus is the eternal Word of God made visible,
approachable, understandable.

We could read all the words
in all the books of theology and spirituality
and not really understand anything.

But when we stand beneath the Cross of Jesus we can say
'This is how much God loved us.'
His secret love's no secret any more.

Seek out the Rock. Where's Peter? And we find Peter today where Peter went after the Resurrection and Pentecost – in Rome. Photograph: Fr Cormac.

Chapter 23

Wisdom is bright, and does not grow dim.
By those who love her she is readily seen.

When the Easter Rising in Ireland failed in 1916,
the authorities were determined to reassert their authority.
The leaders of the Rising were quickly tried and executed.
A generation of leadership was all but obliterated.
And others found themselves picked up
and taken to concentration camps.

One of those arrested was a painter and decorator
called Peadar Kearney.
Not just a workman – he was a man soaked in literature,
English and Irish, and a poet in his own right.
In the year of the Easter Rising one of his poems
was set to music and became enormously popular.
It was *The Soldier's Song* and it's now
the National Anthem of Ireland.

In 1920 Kearney found himself an internee
in a bleak and miserable camp in the north.
And it became his practice to take a constitutional
every evening. He'd walk round the entire periphery
of the camp – about half a mile. And he devised
a very simple way of provoking the authorities.
To every man he met on his walk,
he'd call out in a loud voice "Where's Deegan?"
Now there was in fact no such person in the camp.
But the answer shouted back to him was always
"He's missing. Deegan's missing."
Most of the fellows knew the game and played it.
Some prisoners hadn't a clue and presumed
that some fellow-prisoner had somehow

got beyond the barbed wire and was at large.
And the British military fell for it and became so curious
about this missing Deegan that an armed guard raided
the prisoners' huts looking for him. Imagine that!
Just a name. An Irish version of Lt Kijé.
But if you say it with enough conviction,
you can persuade someone he really exists.

Peadar Kearney did it just to make fools of the authorities.
But people are conned like that all the time.

If you say loudly enough that Armageddon is about to happen
someone will believe it and dive for cover! Where's Deegan?

If you proclaim loudly enough that people whose birthdays
are close together are under the same 'star sign',
there's always someone
who'll allow astrologers to make a living
pretending they know what's going to happen.
Where's Deegan?

And it's particularly likely to happen round religious beliefs.
The history of Christianity is littered
with crackpots and conmen
who have claimed their own personal access to the truth
and have persuaded others to believe them.
When's the Last Day?
When's Armageddon?
Where's the horseman of the Apocalypse?
Where's Deegan?

It's when you realise how weirdly gullible people are
that you thank God for the bright wisdom of the
Catholic Church.
When we hear people talking up this prophet,
or that preacher, or this guru, or that authority;
when we hear those confident shouts of Where's Deegan?
that's when we say quietly: where's Peter?

Our Lord knew how many false prophets and phonies
and oddballs would try to claim his name and his authority.
We only have to look at the splinter-groups and fragmentation
of Christianity to see how schism slips into heresy
and heresy into eccentricity
and eccentricity into the totally barmy.
And all in the name of Jesus.
It can't be right. So how do we *know*?

We recall the promises of Jesus,
that he would not only send the Holy Spirit,
but he would build his Church on a Rock: the Rock of Peter.

So when people get carried away and some cry I'm for Paul
and others I'm for Apollos, the sensible Christian says:
Where's the Rock? Where's Peter?
That's where the real authority lies.

Peter can be recognised because, like Christ his master,
he speaks with authority.
When we need to interpret the signs of the times,
when we want to understand the scriptures,
when we want to choose wisely from all the creeds available,
that's when we say – seek out the Rock. Where's Peter?
And we find Peter today where Peter went
after the Resurrection and Pentecost – in Rome.

We find Peter teaching there now, as then.
The *Catechism of the Catholic Church* today
is like the Epistle of St Peter two thousand years ago.
The present Pope is there, to cut through the delusions
and the gimmicks and the trendy nonsense,
and to put us in touch with the authentic voice of Christ.

Where's Deegan? Deegan's missing.
Yes indeed he is.
Deegan has no root in reality at all. But where's Peter?
Peter is there for us, reliable as ever.

On Tuesday we'll be celebrating the feast
of the dedication of the Lateran basilica.
That's the Pope's Cathedral as Bishop of Rome.
A cathedral is a building that houses the *cathedra,*
the seat of authority from which the bishop
in the apostolic succession teaches.
The *cathedra* of the Bishop of Rome is the rock of Peter.
So in all the clamour and fuss, no one can confuse us.

Where's Deegan? Deegan's missing.
Where's Peter?
Peter is full in the panting heart of Rome,
our rock and our guarantee that Christ's teaching
reaches us as he intended it to.

Wisdom is bright, and does not grow dim.
By those who love her she is readily seen.

Chapter 24

The waters shall never again become a flood
to destroy all things of flesh.

It was an awesome sight to see a bridge
that normally spanned a river
stranded in the middle of a flood.
Both ends disappeared into the waters;
only the bridge itself was above
and it had become a refuge for villagers,
driven out of their poor homes
and camped out on this man-made island.
Nature mocks man's pretensions: man builds a bridge
to master a river and nature laughs in his face
and makes his proud bridge a symbol of his impotence.

Of all the tragic images to come out of Mozambique
these last few days, that bridge to nowhere,
that pathetic remnant of engineering, was the most graphic.
Few things put man in perspective more forcibly
than the cruel sea.
So it's not surprising that one of the great stories
of the Hebrew scriptures focussed on a flood.
The angle was one that would nowadays strike us as odd.
The flood was interpreted as God's anger.
Human beings had been so badly behaved
that God was having second thoughts about creation.
Only Noah stood out, as a faithful man,
and God tipped him off to escape the flood.

In many ways the story of Noah
is like the story of Adam and Eve.
Both stories tell of humans getting uppity –
what my Granny used to call "peas above sticks."

(Gardeners will know that when you sow peas
you need to give them something to climb up.
And if the sticks aren't tall enough the peas
keep on growing with nothing to support them
and fall flat on their face.
Peas above sticks are rather pathetic.
They grow non-stop and then look somewhat foolish
when they over-reach themselves.)

Adam and Eve thought they were so clever
that they knew better than God what was good for them –
peas above sticks.
And it was the same with the people of Noah's time.
"You don't want to waste your life obeying commandments:
eat, drink and be merry – no problem – no one can stop you."
They knew best! Peas above sticks.

And as the writer describes it, God was so miffed
by their stupidity that he said, well, you know –
or think you know – what's best for you
and you think the sun is always going to shine.
So how are you going to cope when the sun disappears
and the storm clouds gather and the monsoons come
and the dry gullies overflow
and the world becomes a vast lake.
How will you drive your Porsches and your Mercs
through real floods?
How will your skyscrapers survive an earthquake?
The Old Testament writers *did* see it as God sending a flood,
as God punishing evil directly.
But that's too easy. And it's dangerous.
Before you know where you are, some smart Alec is saying,
"Those people in Mozambique must have been
dreadful sinners if God is punishing them like that.
Thank God I'm home and dry in Middlesex
and the Almighty gives me his seal of approval."

Such smugness!
Such self-delusion!!
Such judgemental tosh!!!

The floods weren't a conspiracy by God,
they just happened.
But many of those who suffer are those who thought
that they could get along without God: the clever-clever.
Peas above sticks.

When God intervenes it's not to hurl thunderbolts
at the wicked.
When God intervenes,
it is to give comfort to those who trust him.
He intervenes by putting new heart into his own,
giving strength of mind to the holy,
giving his followers the will to survive.
He puts it in the mind of Noah to read the signs
and to take precautions. Noah wasn't peas above sticks.
He was a wise man and he saw global warming coming
and the danger of floods increase, and he very sensibly
made provision for a disaster.

Today there are still terrible floods,
not a punishment from God, but a reminder
of man's littleness in the face of nature.
We have to take care of our world; we abuse it at our peril.
If we destroy the rain forests, if we turn our children
into junkies, if we destroy human life for human gain
and pleasure, we challenge the wisdom of God.

We think we're so clever, but it's peas above sticks
and our pride will come before our fall.
If we run planet earth in harmony with goodness,
and still the floods come,
we will be as safe as Noah's ark,
but if we abuse the earth for greed,
we will drown in a flood of our own making.

It's an old, old story and I've told it
from a slightly different angle, but the message is the same.
The rainbow reminds us that God does not seek to destroy us,
but that we need God, and his love, and his perspective
to live successfully in this world.

How happy those flood-victims in Mozambique would be
if we could really show them
love of God,
love of neighbour,
love of creation,
love of the environment.
We've a long way to go.

When Jesus returned from being tempted in the desert
by Satan, the Prince of Peas-above-sticks,
he didn't say "You're doing a great job, boys,"
he said "Repent, and believe the Good News."

Chapter 25

Women with child, women in labour.

Next week sees a crucial vote in the House of Commons,
on cloning. Not cloning sheep. Human beings.
For some people it's a legitimate development,
and I've no doubt that Dr Evan Harris, the MP
who is introducing the Bill sees it as a technical advance
which will do more good than harm.
It will enable more research to be undertaken
on human embryos and lead to other uses of the embryos,
using them as sources of material to repair
other human beings. It's not an ignoble ambition.
In a way it's like using a dead man's eyes or kidneys.
And we're happy with that.

But the essential difference is that we don't actually
kill the man in order to obtain his eyes or kidneys.

The cloning of embryos is a policy which sets out
to create human life and then to terminate human life.
And for us that is morally unacceptable.

If this legislation goes through, embryos will be created
in test tubes and will be used for research
as if they were spare parts rather than actual human beings.
The scientists don't see them as persons with human rights,
but as human material.
It is the teaching of the Church that fertilising
is the essential act of creation.
Life begins at conception, and science confirms
that key human characteristics are laid down at that moment.
Dr Harris would say that as the embryo develops it is *potentially*
a human person but not actually a human person;
that it only *becomes* a person when he or she is born.

The Church says that once life has begun
no-one has the right to end that life.
Once conceived, the human person is in being
in the womb, in the test tube,
in the labour ward, or in the hospital.
Human life comes into being when an embryo
comes into existence and so to destroy an embryo
is to destroy a human life, to kill a human being.

An embryo is a human person yet unborn.
Any mother knows how the embryo stirs within
and how a human person is growing.
The New Testament relates to that in the story
of John the Baptist, an embryo in his mother's womb,
who leapt for joy when Christ approached.
The life within the mother is as precious
in the eyes of God as the life after birth.

So it is a major tragedy when cloning is allowed
and embryos can be created in laboratories
and used for research and chucked out
when they've served their purpose.
We cannot accept this abuse of human life.
Human life must be respected:
it should begin in the act of love,
it should complete its formation in the womb
and come to birth, and it should be cherished thereafter.
No scientific research, however good its intentions,
can be acceptable if it compromises the value of life itself.
It is not acceptable to create and destroy human life
in laboratories.

To make it sound respectable, it is sometimes referred to
as 'therapeutic cloning.'
Therapeutic for whom?
Certainly not therapeutic for the embryo concerned,
who is created to be exploited and then destroyed.

Earlier this month Archbishop Vincent of Birmingham
wrote a pastoral letter. His diocese includes Oxford
and Dr Harris is one of the MPs for the city,
so the Archbishop needed to alert his flock.
What is being proposed by Dr Harris is that human embryos
can be used and produced by cloning for the sole purpose
of medical experimentation.
"Of course the church recognises that scientific research
is a proper expression of the responsibility
God has given us over his creation,
and that the aim and intention of this research may be good."
"Nevertheless," says the Archbishop, "it is utterly clear that
the means chosen involve the manipulation and destruction
of human life in ways which are totally unacceptable.
A good end does not justify an immoral means."

We need to do more than just pray that this threat
will go away. We are the people and we must
let our representatives know our strength of belief
on this issue.

That biblical phrase "women with child" –
that's what embryo means – a child in its mother's womb.
Humanity at its most defenceless.

*A rainbow over the marsh behind Borth. Illustration by C Rossiter, engraved by Dalziel Brothers. From **Borth Lyrics** by Edward Thring, Uppingham, John Hawthorn, 1881.*

Chapter 26

I set my bow in the clouds and it shall be a sign
of the Covenant between me and the earth

At this stage in her life my mother spends a lot of time
with her eyes closed – not exactly asleep, but just too tired
to keep them open.
But even though she looks asleep, she isn't
and I've discovered that she enjoys hearing
some of the poems she learnt eighty years ago
when she was a girl. Quite often she joins in –
with her eyes still shut, but the memory ticking over nicely.
The other day I was reading an old favourite
by Christina Rossetti:

There are bridges on the rivers, as pretty as you please,
But the bow that bridges heaven and overtops the trees,
And builds a road from earth to sky is prettier far than these.

The bow that bridges heaven – how much the rainbow
appeals to our imagination.
The Americans belt out about it.
Judy Garland expects a fantasy fairyland
at the end of the yellow brick road,
somewhere over the rainbow.
The Irish are more whimsical.
Finian's Rainbow takes us into a mythology
where the end of the rainbow indicates the hiding place
of a crock of gold.
But of course it's not that cold hard metal they mean by gold,
but the gold of happiness.
The rainbow is a symbol of hopefulness in the Scriptures,
because it is something which touches both earth and heaven.
God seems to show us a bridge linking two places
with his presence:

one end in the Republic, the other in the six counties;
one end in the white man's suburbs,
the other in the black man's township.
God makes his beautiful bridge shimmering in the sky
and every time we build a bridge to someone else
we do God's work.

Last week a young soldier checking a driver's documents
smiled at the young woman driving the car,
building a bridge from his people to hers.
And at that very moment he was struck down
by a murderous bullet.
His death was a human tragedy, because
his smile and his courtesy was human hope.
The woman who saw that smile will be inspired by it
for the rest of her life, and through her words
it will be an inspiration to us too.
Hatred and murder will pass into oblivion,
but those who in their own individual way use courtesy
and friendliness to begin to build bridges
have an undying place in heaven.

Murder seems to have blotted out a young life
just as storm clouds blot out the sun,
but it is against the blackest of clouds
that the rainbow speaks most powerfully of hope.
If the world remembers that soldier's smile
trying to build bridges, he will have triumphed
over the bullet that killed him.
The building of bridges is God's work
and death and destruction are the work of the devil.
The rainbow isn't a fairy story, it's an inspiration
and it is up to every one of us to be a builder of bridges.

   The bow that bridges heaven and overtops the trees
   And builds a road from earth to sky is prettier far than these.

Chapter 27

A time of great distress.

We are living our lives in a time of great distress,
a time of floundering in moral and spiritual uncertainties.
For many of our contemporaries there is a complete absence
of a moral landscape.
It's not that people are wickedly doing wrong,
but that they don't have a clue
what is wrong and what is right.
A book was published recently about the Caroline Beale case.
She was the thirty-year-old woman who concealed her pregnancy
even from her boyfriend and gave birth to her baby in a
New York hotel room and then tried to smuggle the body
out of America in her luggage. It was a bizarre episode.
And it revealed a great deal about the absence
of moral values which makes this such a time of distress.
The American courts allowed a charge of murder
to be reduced to manslaughter,
but even a charge of manslaughter outraged a lot of people
who saw the mother as a victim
and her baby as part of her predicament.
Now of course one *must* feel much sympathy for the woman,
because she had clearly had no moral map to help her
on her way through life.
The father of the child, who'd been living with her
for eight years, walked out when she was arrested
and never contacted her again.
Yes – she certainly demands our compassion.

When Libby Purves was reviewing the book in *The Times*
she could not but notice the moral vacuum in which
the woman lived, a moral universe without any semblance
of beliefs or values, a frightening spiritual void.

She described the book as a portrait "of functional,
employable thirty-somethings who are nonetheless
morally illiterate on great issues."
The woman herself while on bail was given shelter
by a warm religious family, but she was inclined to sneer
at their religious values.
"Religion," she said, "is something people turn to
when they have nothing else."

I'm sure that's how she and many others like her see life.
They exist simply for themselves and for their own feelings,
and they live apparently happily enough
in a life unshaped by any depth of thought about others,
or by any coherent view of the values of life.

Reading the book about the case convinced Libby Purves
that the real hero was the often-criticised
American system of justice.
The Americans had to put up with a lot of flak
for daring to assert that allowing a new-born baby to die
is an absolute wrong.
The District Attorney said at one point: "In the United States
you don't get extra points for killing a baby."

Now of course a sick woman, unsupported
by any strong moral sense, does not belong in prison
but that consideration of mercy should not eclipse
the terrible wrong that had been done.

Religion isn't the last resort of the pathetic;
it's the primary awareness of humanity that life
is a gift from God, which needs to be protected
when it is at its most weak and vulnerable.
The American system, for all its faults, spoke for the weak,
spoke up firmly for the baby that had been irresponsibly created
and then thoughtlessly put to death.

The reaction of parts of the British press was
a sentimental sympathy for the woman,
ignoring the sympathy to which the baby was entitled.
And that should make us uneasy because life
isn't about the survival of the strongest;
it's about the rights of all.
Life isn't the plaything of the affluent;
it is a gift from God.

When the moral stature of this time of distress
comes to be judged by history, history will point
to the tragic corpses of children and ask
how their lives came to be held so cheap.
That particular case was a tragedy for all concerned –
and what it revealed was a moral climate
in which people are growing up without any real sense
of the value of human life.

Our faith could never go along with a policy
of disposable babies.
Our faith perceives each and every human being
as a child of God.
That is not the religion of those 'who have nothing else.'
That is the religion of those who are morally certain
that nothing is as valuable to humanity
as love, relationships, family, fulfilment,
and that the creation of new life
is the greatest of all blessings.

The popes are the cat's-eyes along the 2000 year road of Christian history. I have a great affection for and devotion to Pope Pius XII. He had studied for a year at the Capranica College, and 63 years later revisited it as Pope. The Vatican issued stamps to mark the visit.

Chapter 28

On this rock I will build my Church.

Gregory was a Roman nobleman,
his father one of the Senators.
And way back in the year 573, Gregory
was perceived to be a young man of such ability
that he was made Prefect of the City of Rome.

The Roman empire had dominated the world for centuries –
its roads and fortifications reached up as far as Hadrian's Wall,
and its armies were strengthened by numbers of slaves
recruited from the peoples conquered by the empire.
The capital, Rome, was rich beyond belief
and so young Gregory had it made.
But Gregory was also a Christian – it had been legal
to be a Christian since the time of Constantine.
Christianity was no longer a forbidden faith
lurking in the catacombs, and was able to attract
many among the idealistic Roman youth.
So Gregory decided that he would abandon
his prosperous public career and dedicate his life to Christ.
He sold his properties and invested the money
in relief of the poor.
He also endowed six monasteries in Sicily
and then a seventh in Rome itself, dedicated to St Andrew.
And he went into that Roman monastery himself,
to live the austere life of a monk.

And that might have been the end of the story,
if several years later the Pope had not winkled him
out of his monastery so he could be one of the
seven deacons of Rome.

In the year 585 he became abbot of his former monastery,
St Andrew's. One day Abbot Gregory went down to the
slave market where the captive victims of the empire were
herded together in pens, human beings up for sale as slaves.
Gregory looked at them all with great compassion –
men, women and children from the Mediterranean
and from Africa; but one little group stood out.

Most of the slaves were dark-eyed, black-haired,
southern types.
But this little group of teenage boys was different –
fair-headed and blue-eyed.
Who are those? asked Gregory.
The trader told him – Angli, from Angleland, England.
Angli? said Gregory. No, not Angli but angeli,
not angles but angels.

He never forgot those boys,
"Those lovely lads once, wet-fresh windfalls of war's storm,"
and when five years later Gregory was elected Bishop
of Rome, he remembered them again
and tried to do something for their country.
He got hold of the prior of St Andrew's,
an Italian called Agostino, and asked him to take a group
of about forty missionaries to England.

Agostino found it a tremendous upheaval but in the summer of 597,
exactly fourteen hundred years ago,
he landed in Kent and set up his headquarters at Canterbury.
He seems to have relied very heavily on advice from Pope Gregory.
Both men died in the same year 604 – the great pope
and the brave prior he sent to the land of the Angli.
That is how Christianity took root again in England,
so we have good reason to be grateful to Bishop Gregory.

He's one of a handful of the popes to be titled 'Great':
Gregory the Great.
There have been fifteen other popes called Gregory, including

the one who gives his name to the Gregorian Calendar.
We think of them today, the feast of St Peter.
because all those Gregories like all those Leos and Piuses,
all those Johns and Benedicts, were all successors of Peter.
Nearly three hundred of them
establish a chain of authority
from Peter himself down to Benedict XVI.
The popes are the cat's-eyes along the two-thousand-year road
of Christian history. They have included great men and small,
splendid saints and bizarre sinners,
but all have helped create the link
which we call the apostolic succession.
England owes its reconversion to Gregory the Great,
but many other popes have influenced our history.
When we celebrate St Peter we celebrate all his successors too –
the Rocks on which the Catholic Church is founded.

Monstrance at the church at Drumshanbo.

The Franciscan nuns in Drumshanbo, County Leitrim, centre their whole life on perpetual adoration of the Blessed Sacrament. Our Lord is never alone. The Poor Clares' commitment to this round-the-clock watching in front of the monstrance began in London in 1857. Their poverty forced them to move from place to place, from England to Ireland. They came to Drumshanbo in 1864. Adoremus in Aeternum.

Chapter 29

Look, all these years I've slaved for you
and never once disobeyed your orders,

If you go to Vienna and take a walk through the inner city
you'll discover that the very centre of the city
is enclosed within a wide and spacious Ring.
The Ring is a circle of wide tree-planted streets
and they are now the complete opposite
of what they were years ago.
In the nineteenth century, in Paris as well as Vienna,
the old city walls were demolished and new
tree-lined boulevards replaced them.

In Vienna the fortifications had formed a protective circle
two-and-a-half miles in circumference, and sixty yards wide.
So when a more settled and prosperous century decided
they weren't needed any more, they made way
for today's spacious and beautiful Ring.
And no less a person than Johann Strauss wrote
one of his best ballroom numbers to mark the event:
The Demolition-Polka; all Vienna danced to it to celebrate
the change from a Ring of walls to a Ring of open space.

But we shouldn't forget that those massive walls
had served their purpose defending the city
from the thirteenth to the nineteenth century.
Twice those massive walls were pounded by Turkish guns,
and the citizens of Vienna defended them desperately
to prevent Moslem forces from sweeping away
the Austrian Empire.

Twice Europe came within an inch of being successfully
invaded by the Turks – and if that had succeeded
St Stephen's Cathedral and other great Cathedrals
of Austria and Germany could well now be mosques
like Santa Sophia in Istanbul.
But the walls of Vienna withstood the onslaught –
and here's the interesting bit.
The cost of building those walls way, way back
was tremendous; but the Duke of Austria had a lucky windfall
which enabled him to pay for it.

He was able to use the money paid by England
to ransom the captive King Richard the Lion-Heart.
The English King had gone crusading
to free the Holy Land from the Saracens
and on the way back he was captured and held prisoner.
A huge ransom had to be raised to pay for his release.
What an irony that all that money, a King's ransom,
was actually used to defend Europe against invasion
by the Turks.

I think about this when I hear the story
of the Prodigal Son's brother.
You can just hear the resentment in his reaction.
'I've slaved for you all these years and done all you wanted
and got nothing for it, and this reprobate does damn all
and you welcome him back with open arms.'

In a similar way you could hear the resentment in England
against paying the King's ransom –
'We've paid enough taxes without having to pay extra
for that – why should we cough up again
just to release that crackpot crusader?'

Resentment is such a waste of emotional energy
and yet how often we find ourselves taking the short view,
full of resentment.

And when we do that it's worth asking ourselves
why we're so het-up about it.
The eventual outcome is beyond our knowledge
so why get agitated? In the fullness of time
the providence of God will sort things out.

The ransom that was taken from resentful Englishmen
eventually saved the whole of Europe from being overrun
and that elegant spacious Ring in Vienna is the reminder of it.

The welcome that was given to the returning Prodigal,
so much against the feelings of his resentful brother,
was the eloquent evidence of the Father's power to forgive.
How much more positive the brother could have been
if he had been able to set aside his resentment
and take on board the great message of forgiveness.

Our happiness as Christians depends on the willingness
of the Father to forgive every single one of us.

No resentment when he forgives others.
Just deep gratitude that he does forgive us.

*On the day that he received his doctorate, Fr Cormac (on right)
is joined outside the Sheldonian by his mother and his cousin,
Fr Austin McCormack, OFM.*

Chapter 30

The way you think is not God's way.

"If I ruled the world, every day would be
the first day of Spring . . . "
Remember it?
One of those wonderfully cheerful songs made popular
by Harry Secombe.
It would be very curmudgeonly to attack it.
"Every heart would have a new song to sing . . ."

You'd have to be a real old misery-guts if you're
going to take exception to such Pickwickian good nature.
It would indeed be a much happier world
if there were more Harry Secombes in it.
And yet we all know in our heart of hearts
that there's a danger in such easy optimism.
Get real. Tell it as it is.
We do need cheerfulness, happiness, innocence –
but we don't need to be facile.

I do share Sir Harry's enjoyment of the First Day of Spring –
but right now there's a nip in the air,
the leaves are just beginning to turn
and the Michaelmas daisies are telling us
that we're on the brink of autumn.
And I *love* the autumn.
Is there any more season more breathtakingly beautiful?
I love to go out to Blenheim when the leaves have turned
but not yet fallen and to marvel at all those yellows and golds,
bronzes and copper reflected in the lake.
One of the joys of living in this country is that all seasons
have their charms – a soggy afternoon suddenly clearing
to a brilliant blue sky and a sensational sunset.

Let's be honest: if every day really was made
the first day of spring we'd get sick to death of daffodils.

There is a cycle in nature: a birth, a flourishing,
a fading and a fall.
If I ruled the world I would encourage everyone
to cherish *all* the seasons, and to delight
in the whole of God's creation.
Not just the First Day of Spring,
but even the Winter Solstice itself.

Real happiness lies in our capacity to enjoy each day
as it comes, and to use each and every day
to increase the amount of love in the world.
How?
Well – it's lovely to chatter with our friends
full of the joys of spring, but it's also a good idea
to chatter happily with the elderly who are far advanced
into the autumn of their lives and suffer from loneliness.
Do we cultivate the spring in our own step
and leave them to moulder?
Or do we try to bring the sunshine into their lives?
Our temptation is always to blot out reality and to pretend
that everything in the garden is always lovely.

St Peter is doing precisely that in the gospel.
Jesus, the realist, was alerting his disciples
to the problems ahead.
And Peter, dear kindly old thing, says
"Oh no no, these things won't happen to you.
You'll be fine."
And Jesus really slaps him down quite hard:
"Get behind me Satan.
You're an obstacle in my path, because your way of thinking
is not God's way, but man's."
Man wants easy answers and quick fixes.

Global warming?
Well that's for Blair and Bush to sort.
Lung cancer? Well it probably won't happen to me.
I'll just keep on with the fags.
Facile. Irresponsible. Foolish. Typical of us.

Jesus expects us to look ahead, realistically.
The pattern of the seasons is part of our existence.
We must look ahead.
We sow so that we can reap.
We harvest so that we can eat in winter.
We take thought for the morrow.
It's *not* always the first day of spring,
but every day brings its own potential,
its own capacity for real joy.
We must use our todays to safeguard our tomorrows.

There is one other final thought.
In nature, the cycles follow one another, again and again.
In each of our lives, yours and mine, there is only one cycle.

My spring is long ago; I loved it; I used it well;
it is a source of many happy memories, but it is gone for ever.

My summer was wonderful; I worked at full throttle;
I took every chance I was given; I lived life to the full
and I'm grateful it lasted so long.

I enjoyed my autumn too: the slowing down
and also the maturity, the ability to reflect
on all that had gone before,
the wonderful joys of shared reminiscences.

And now in retirement the days are shortening.
And of all the seasons, it's the one where taking up the cross
has its own inevitability: the pills and injections,
the lack of energy.

And it's now that the truth strikes home.
Humanly speaking, there will be no second spring.
Like the leaves, I will fall.
But unlike the leaves, I do not lose my identity;
I do not simply recycle.
And Harry Secombe is right after all.

Death takes us through that door into a First Day of Spring
which does indeed last for ever.
Not an endlessly repeated boring first day –
but the infinite number of ways of experiencing
the love of God in eternity.

I was given one spring, one summer, one autumn, one winter –
and when the Son of Man comes
he will reward each one of us according to our behaviour.

It's the way we *live* our lives, day after day,
the way we colour our lives
that 'stains the white radiance of Eternity'.

And so, back to the Library. The view from the east end of the beautiful groves of St John's College, Oxford, looking towards the College Library. It was built by William Laud, later Archbishop of Canterbury. Like the founder, Sir Thomas White, he is buried in the College chapel. The gardens have since 1958 provided me with a blessed sense of peace and calm. "I think if I were ever hurt or disquieted, I should only have to go there, or even imagine them, to feel quiet again." (diary, 4 August 1965).